VERY SHORT INTRODUCTIONS are for anyone wanting a stimulating and accessible way in to a new subject. They are written by experts, and have been published in more than 25 languages worldwide.

The series began in 1995, and now represents a wide variety of topics in history, philosophy, religion, science, and the humanities. Over the next few years it will grow to a library of around 200 volumes – a Very Short Introduction to everything from ancient Egypt and Indian philosophy to conceptual art and cosmology.

Very Short Introductions available now:

ANCIENT PHILOSOPHY
    Julia Annas
THE ANGLO-SAXON AGE
    John Blair
ANIMAL RIGHTS   David DeGrazia
ARCHAEOLOGY   Paul Bahn
ARCHITECTURE
    Andrew Ballantyne
ARISTOTLE   Jonathan Barnes
ART HISTORY   Dana Arnold
ART THEORY   Cynthia Freeland
THE HISTORY OF
    ASTRONOMY   Michael Hoskin
ATHEISM   Julian Baggini
AUGUSTINE   Henry Chadwick
BARTHES   Jonathan Culler
THE BIBLE   John Riches
BRITISH POLITICS
    Anthony Wright
BUDDHA   Michael Carrithers
BUDDHISM   Damien Keown
CAPITALISM   James Fulcher
THE CELTS   Barry Cunliffe
CHOICE THEORY
    Michael Allingham
CHRISTIAN ART   Beth Williamson
CLASSICS   Mary Beard and
    John Henderson
CLAUSEWITZ   Michael Howard
THE COLD WAR
    Robert McMahon

CONTINENTAL PHILOSOPHY
    Simon Critchley
COSMOLOGY   Peter Coles
CRYPTOGRAPHY
    Fred Piper and Sean Murphy
DADA AND SURREALISM
    David Hopkins
DARWIN   Jonathan Howard
DEMOCRACY   Bernard Crick
DESCARTES   Tom Sorell
DRUGS   Leslie Iversen
THE EARTH   Martin Redfern
EGYPTIAN MYTHOLOGY
    Geraldine Pinch
EIGHTEENTH-CENTURY
    BRITAIN   Paul Langford
THE ELEMENTS   Philip Ball
EMOTION   Dylan Evans
EMPIRE   Stephen Howe
ENGELS   Terrell Carver
ETHICS   Simon Blackburn
THE EUROPEAN UNION
    John Pinder
EVOLUTION
    Brian and Deborah Charlesworth
FASCISM   Kevin Passmore
THE FRENCH REVOLUTION
    William Doyle
FREUD   Anthony Storr
GALILEO   Stillman Drake
GANDHI   Bhikhu Parekh

Available soon:

AFRICAN HISTORY
John Parker and Richard Rathbone
ANCIENT EGYPT Ian Shaw
THE BRAIN Michael O'Shea
BUDDHIST ETHICS
Damien Keown
CHAOS Leonard Smith
CHRISTIANITY Linda Woodhead
CITIZENSHIP Richard Bellamy
CLASSICAL ARCHITECTURE
Robert Tavernor
CLONING Arlene Judith Klotzko
CONTEMPORARY ART
Julian Stallabrass
THE CRUSADES
Christopher Tyerman
DERRIDA Simon Glendinning
DESIGN John Heskett
DINOSAURS David Norman
DREAMING J. Allan Hobson
ECONOMICS Partha Dasgupta
THE END OF THE WORLD
Bill McGuire
EXISTENTIALISM Thomas Flynn
THE FIRST WORLD WAR
Michael Howard
FREE WILL Thomas Pink
FUNDAMENTALISM
Malise Ruthven
HABERMAS Gordon Finlayson

HIEROGLYPHS
Penelope Wilson
HIROSHIMA B. R. Tomlinson
HUMAN EVOLUTION
Bernard Wood
INTERNATIONAL RELATIONS
Paul Wilkinson
JAZZ Brian Morton
MANDELA Tom Lodge
MEDICAL ETHICS
Tony Hope
THE MIND Martin Davies
MYTH Robert Segal
NATIONALISM Steven Grosby
PERCEPTION Richard Gregory
PHILOSOPHY OF RELIGION
Jack Copeland and Diane Proudfoot
PHOTOGRAPHY
Steve Edwards
THE RAJ Denis Judd
THE RENAISSANCE
Jerry Brotton
RENAISSANCE ART
Geraldine Johnson
SARTRE Christina Howells
THE SPANISH CIVIL WAR
Helen Graham
TRAGEDY Adrian Poole
THE TWENTIETH CENTURY
Martin Conway

For more information visit our web site

www.oup.co.uk/vsi

Manfred B. Steger

GLOBALIZATION

A Very Short Introduction

OXFORD
UNIVERSITY PRESS

OXFORD
UNIVERSITY PRESS

Great Clarendon Street, Oxford OX2 6DP

Oxford University Press is a department of the University of Oxford.
It furthers the University's objective of excellence in research, scholarship,
and education by publishing worldwide in

Oxford New York

Auckland Bangkok Buenos Aires Cape Town Chennai
Dar es Salaam Delhi Hong Kong Istanbul Karachi Kolkata
Kuala Lumpur Madrid Melbourne Mexico City Mumbai Nairobi
São Paulo Shanghai Taipei Tokyo Toronto

Oxford is a registered trade mark of Oxford University Press
in the UK and in certain other countries

Published in the United States
by Oxford University Press Inc., New York

© Manfred B. Steger 2003

British Library Cataloguing in Publication Data
Data available

Library of Congress Cataloging in Publication Data
Data available

ISBN 13: 978-0-19-280359-7
ISBN 10: 0-19-280359-X

9 10

Typeset by RefineCatch Ltd, Bungay, Suffolk
Printed in Great Britain by
Ashford Colour Press Ltd., Gosport, Hampshire

*For my students at Illinois State University
and the University of Hawai'i-Manoa.*

Contents

Preface

It is a daunting task to write a short, accessible introduction to such a complex topic as 'globalization'. This challenge becomes even more formidable in the case of a *very short* introduction. Hence, it is not surprising that the authors of the few existing short introductions to the subject have opted to discuss only one aspect of globalization – usually the emerging global economic system, its history, structure, and supposed benefits and failings. While helpful in explaining the intricacies of international trade policy, global financial markets, worldwide flows of goods, services, and labour, transnational corporations, offshore financial centres, foreign direct investment, and the new international economic institutions, such narrow accounts often leave the general reader with a shallow understanding of globalization as primarily an economic phenomenon.

To be sure, the discussion of economic matters must be a significant part of any comprehensive account of globalization, but the latter should not be conflated with the former. The present volume makes the case that globalization is best thought of as a multidimensional set of social processes that resists being confined to any single thematic framework. Indeed, the transformative powers of globalization reach deeply into the economic, political, cultural, technological, and ecological dimensions of contemporary social life.

In addition, globalization contains important *discursive* aspects in the form of ideologically charged narratives that put before the public a particular agenda of topics for discussion, questions to ask, and claims to make. The existence of these narratives shows that globalization is not merely an objective process, but also a plethora of stories that define, describe, and analyse that very process. The social forces behind these competing accounts of globalization seek to endow this relatively new buzzword with norms, values, and meanings that not only legitimate and advance specific power interests, but also shape the personal and collective identities of billions of people. In order to shed light on these rhetorical manoeuvres, any introduction to globalization ought to examine its ideological dimension. After all, it is mostly the question of whether globalization ought to be considered a 'good' or a 'bad' thing that has spawned heated debates in classrooms, boardrooms, and on the streets.

This book has been written with a keen awareness that the study of globalization falls outside currently established academic fields. Yet, the lack of a firm disciplinary home also contains great opportunity. 'Globalization studies' is emerging as a new field that cuts across traditional disciplinary boundaries. This strong emphasis on interdisciplinarity requires students of globalization to familiarize themselves with literatures on subjects that have often been studied in isolation from each other. The greatest challenge facing today's globalization researcher lies, therefore, in connecting and synthesizing the various strands of knowledge in a way that does justice to the increasingly fluid and interdependent nature of our postmodern world. In short, globalization studies calls for an interdisciplinary approach broad enough to behold the 'big picture'. Such a comprehensive intellectual enterprise may well lead to the rehabilitation of the academic generalist whose status, for too long, has been overshadowed by the specialist.

Finally, let me add a word of clarification. While the main purpose of this book lies in providing its audience with a descriptive and explanatory account of the various dimensions of globalization, the careful reader will detect throughout the chapters a critical undertone.

However, my sceptical perspective on the nature and the effects of contemporary forms of globalization should not be interpreted as a blanket rejection of the phenomenon itself. I believe that we should take comfort in the fact that the world is becoming a more interdependent place that enhances people's chances to recognize and acknowledge their common humanity. I welcome the progressive transformation of social structures that goes by the name of globalization, provided that the global flow of ideas and commodities, and the rapid development of technology, go hand in hand with greater forms of freedom and equality for all people, as well as with more effective protection of our global environment. The brunt of my critique is directed at particular manifestations and tendencies of globalization that strike me as being at odds with the noble cosmopolitan vision of a more egalitarian and less violent global order.

It is a pleasant duty to record my debts of gratitude. First, I want to thank my colleagues and friends at the Globalization Research Center at the University of Hawai'i-Manoa for their consistent support of my research agenda. Special thanks are also due to my colleagues at Illinois State University, particularly Jamal Nassar and Lane Crothers, for their willingness to read parts of the manuscript and offer helpful suggestions. I am grateful to Kay Stults, a graphic designer at ISU, for her excellent work on the maps. I also want to express my deep appreciation to numerous readers, reviewers, and audiences around the world, who, over several years, made insightful comments in response to my public lectures and publications on the subject of globalization.

I am grateful to Eldon Wegner, chair of the department of sociology at the University of Hawai'i-Manoa, for his efforts to provide me with valuable office space as well as with the opportunity to teach relevant summer courses in social theory. I also appreciate the enthusiastic research assistance provided by my graduate assistant Ryan Canney.

Franz J. Broswimmer, a wonderful friend and hard-working research specialist at the Globalization Research Center in Honolulu, deserves special recognition. He supplied me with valuable information on the ecological and historical aspects of globalization. Shelley Cox, my editor at Oxford University Press, has been a shining example of professionalism and competence. Finally, as always, I want to thank my wife, Perle Besserman, for her untiring support. Many people have contributed to improving the quality of this book; its remaining flaws are my own responsibility.

Abbreviations

AOL	America Online
APEC	Asian Pacific Economic Cooperation
ASEAN	Association of South East Asian Nations
BCE	Before the Common Era
CE	Common Era
CEO	Chief Executive Officer
CFCs	Chlorofluorocarbons
CITES	Convention on International Trade in Endangered Species of Wild Flora and Fauna
CNN	Cable News Network
CNBC	Cable National Broadcasting Corporation
EU	European Union
FTAA	Free Trade Area of the Americas
G8	Group of Eight
GATT	General Agreement of Tariffs and Trade
GDP	Gross domestic product
GNP	Gross national product
INGO	International non-governmental organization
IMF	International Monetary Fund
MAI	Multilateral Agreement on Investment
MERCOSUR	*Mercado Comun del Sur* (Southern Common Market)
MTV	Music Television
NAFTA	North American Free Trade Agreement

NATO	North Atlantic Treaty Organization
NGO	Non-governmental organization
OECD	Organization for Economic Cooperation and Development
OPEC	Organization of Petroleum Exporting Countries
TNCs	Transnational Corporations
UN	United Nations
UNESCO	United Nations Educational, Scientific and Cultural Organization
WTO	World Trade Organization

List of illustrations

List of maps

Chapter 1
Globalization: a contested concept

In the autumn of 2001, I was teaching an undergraduate class on modern political and social theory. Still traumatized by the recent terrorist attacks on the World Trade Center and the Pentagon, most of my students couldn't quite grasp the connection between the violent forces of religious fundamentalism and the more secular picture of a technologically sophisticated, rapidly globalizing world that I had sought to convey in class lectures and discussions. 'I understand that "globalization" is a contested concept that refers to sometimes contradictory social processes,' a bright history major at the back of the room quipped, 'but how can you say that the TV image of a religious fanatic who denounces modernity and secularism from a mountain cave in Afghanistan perfectly captures the complex dynamics of globalization? Don't these terrible acts of terrorism suggest the opposite, namely, the growth of parochial forces that undermine globalization?' Obviously, the student was referring to Saudi-born Al Qaeda leader Osama bin Laden, whose videotaped statement condemning the activities of 'international infidels' had been broadcast worldwide on 7 October.

Struck by the sense of intellectual urgency that fuelled my student's question, I realized that the story of globalization would remain elusive without real-life examples capable of breathing shape, colour, and sound into a vague concept that had become *the*

1

buzzword of our time. Hence, before delving into necessary matters of definition and analytical clarification, we ought to approach our subject in less abstract fashion. I suggest we begin our journey with a careful examination of the aforementioned videotape. It will soon become fairly obvious why a deconstruction of those images provides important clues to the nature and dynamics of the phenomenon we have come to call 'globalization'.

Deconstructing Osama bin Laden

The infamous videotape bears no date, but experts estimate that the recording was made less than two weeks before it was broadcast. The timing of its release appears to have been carefully planned so as to achieve the maximum effect on the day the United States commenced its bombing campaign against Taliban and Al Qaeda ('The Base') forces in Afghanistan. Although Osama bin Laden and his top lieutenants were then hiding in a remote region of the country, they obviously possessed the hi-tech equipment needed to record the statement. Moreover, Al Qaeda members clearly enjoyed immediate access to sophisticated information and telecommunication networks that kept them informed – in real-time – of relevant international developments. Bin Laden may have denounced the forces of modernity with great conviction, but the smooth operation of his entire organization was entirely dependent on advanced forms of technology developed in the last two decades of the 20th century.

To further illustrate this apparent contradiction, consider the complex chain of global interdependencies that must have existed in order for bin Laden's message to be heard and seen by billions of TV viewers around the world. After making its way from the secluded mountains of eastern Afghanistan to the capital city of Kabul, the videotape was dropped off by an unknown courier outside the local office of Al-Jazeera, a Qatar-based television company. This network had been launched only five years earlier as

1. Al Qaeda leader Osama bin Laden addressing a global audience on 7 October 2001.

a state-financed, Arabic-language news and current affairs channel that offered limited programming. Before the founding of Al-Jazeera, cutting-edge TV journalism – such as free-ranging public affairs interviews and talk shows with call-in audiences – simply did not exist in the Arab world. Within only three years, however, Al-Jazeera was offering its Middle Eastern audience a dizzying array of programmes, transmitted around the clock by powerful satellites put into orbit by European rockets and American space shuttles.

Indeed, the network's market share increased even further as a result of the dramatic reduction in the price and size of satellite dishes. Suddenly, such technologies became affordable, even for low-income consumers. By the turn of the century, Al-Jazeera broadcasts could be watched around the clock on all five continents. In 2001, the company further intensified its global reach when its chief executives signed a lucrative cooperation agreement with CNN, the leading news network owned by the giant multinational corporation AOL-Time-Warner. A few months later, when the world's attention shifted to the war in Afghanistan, Al-Jazeera had already positioned itself as a truly global player, powerful enough to rent equipment to such prominent news providers as Reuters and ABC, sell satellite time to the Associated Press and BBC, and design an innovative Arabic-language business news channel together with its other American network partner, CNBC.

Unhampered by national borders and geographical obstacles, cooperation among these sprawling news networks had become so efficient that CNN acquired and broadcast a copy of the Osama bin Laden tape only a few hours after it had been delivered to the Al-Jazeera office in Kabul. Caught off guard by the incredible speed of today's information exchange, the Bush administration asked the Qatari government to 'rein in Al-Jazeera', claiming that the swift airing of the bin Laden tape without prior consultation was contributing to the rise of anti-American sentiments in the Arab world and thus threatened to undermine the US war effort. However, not only was the perceived 'damage' already done, but segments of the tape – including the full text of bin Laden's statement – could be viewed online by anyone with access to a computer and a modem. The Al-Jazeera website quickly attracted an international audience as its daily hit count skyrocketed to over seven million.

There can be no doubt that it was the existence of this chain of global interdependencies and interconnections that made possible the instant broadcast of bin Laden's speech to a global audience. At the same time, however, it must be emphasized that even those voices that oppose modernity cannot extricate themselves from the very process of globalization they so decry. In order to spread their message and recruit new sympathizers, antimodernizers must utilize the tools provided by globalization. This obvious truth was visible even in bin Laden's personal appearance. The tape shows that he was wearing contemporary military fatigues over traditional Arab garments. In other words, his dress reflects the contemporary processes of fragmentation and cross-fertilization that globalization scholars call 'hybridization' – the mixing of different cultural forms and styles facilitated by global economic and cultural exchanges. In fact, the pale colours of bin Laden's mottled combat dress betrayed its Russian origins, suggesting that he wore the jacket as a symbolic reminder of the fierce guerrilla war waged by him and other Islamic militants against the Soviet occupation forces in Afghanistan during the 1980s. His ever-present AK-47 Kalashnikov, too, was probably made in Russia, although dozens of gun factories around the world have been building this popular assault rifle for over 40 years. By the mid-1990s, more than 70 million Kalashnikovs had been manufactured in Russia and abroad. At least 50 national armies include such rifles in their arsenal, making Kalashnikovs truly weapons of global choice. Thus, bin Laden's AK-47 could have come from anywhere in the world. However, given the astonishing globalization of organized crime during the last two decades, it is quite conceivable that bin Laden's rifle was part of an illegal arms deal hatched and executed by such powerful international criminal organizations as Al Qaeda and the Russian Mafia. It is also possible that the rifle arrived in Afghanistan by means of an underground arms trade similar to the one that surfaced in May 1996, when police in San Francisco seized 2,000 illegally imported AK-47s manufactured in China.

A close look at bin Laden's right wrist reveals yet another clue to the powerful dynamics of globalization. As he directs his words of contempt for the United States and its allies at his hand-held microphone, his retreating sleeve exposes a stylish sports watch. Journalists who noticed this expensive accessory have speculated about the origins of the timepiece in question. The emerging consensus points to a Timex product. However, given that Timex watches are as American as apple pie, it seems rather ironic that the Al Qaeda leader should have chosen this particular chronometer. After all, Timex Corporation, originally the Waterbury Clock Company, was founded in the 1850s in Connecticut's Naugatuck Valley, known throughout the 19th century as the 'Switzerland of America'. Today, the company has gone multinational, maintaining close relations to affiliated businesses and sales offices in 65 countries. The corporation employs 7,500 employees, located on four continents. Thousands of workers – mostly from low-wage countries in the global South – constitute the driving force behind Timex's global production process.

Our brief deconstruction of some of the central images on the videotape makes it easier to understand why the seemingly anachronistic images of an antimodern terrorist in front of an Afghan cave do, in fact, capture some essential dynamics of globalization. Indeed, the tensions between the forces of particularism and those of universalism have reached unprecedented levels only because interdependencies that connect the local to the global have been growing faster than at any time in history. The rise of international terrorist organizations like Al Qaeda represents but one of the many manifestations of globalization. Just as bin Laden's romantic ideology of a 'pure Islam' is itself the result of the modern imagination, so has our global age with its obsession for technology and its mass-market commodities indelibly shaped the violent backlash against globalization.

Our deconstruction of Osama bin Laden has provided us with a real-life example of the intricate – and sometimes contradictory – social dynamics of globalization. We are now in a better position to tackle the rather demanding task of assembling a working definition of globalization that brings some analytical precision to a contested concept that has proven to be notoriously hard to pin down.

Toward a definition of globalization

Since its earliest appearance in the 1960s, the term 'globalization' has been used in both popular and academic literature to describe a process, a condition, a system, a force, and an age. Given that these competing labels have very different meanings, their indiscriminate usage is often obscure and invites confusion. For example, a sloppy conflation of process and condition encourages circular definitions that possess little explanatory power. For example, the often-repeated truism that 'globalization [the process] leads to more globalization [the condition]' does not allow us to draw meaningful analytical distinctions between causes and effects. Hence, I suggest that we use the term *globality* to signify a *social condition* characterized by the existence of global economic, political, cultural, and environmental interconnections and flows that make many of the currently existing borders and boundaries irrelevant. Yet, we should not assume that 'globality' refers to a determinate endpoint that precludes any further development. Rather, this concept points to a particular social condition that, like all conditions, is destined to give way to new, qualitatively distinct constellations. For example, it is conceivable that globality might be transformed into something we could call 'planetarity' – a new social formation brought about by the successful colonization of our solar system. Moreover, we could easily imagine different social manifestations of globality: one might be based primarily on values of individualism and competition, as well as on an economic system of private property, while another might embody more communal and cooperative social arrangements, including less capitalistic economic relations. These possible alternatives point to the fundamentally *indeterminate character* of globality; it is likely that our great-grandchildren will have a better sense of which alternative is likely to win out.

Conversely, the term *globalization* should be used to refer to a *set of social processes* that are thought to transform our present social condition into one of globality. At its core, then, globalization is about shifting forms of human contact. Indeed, the popular phrase 'globalization is happening' contains three important pieces of information: first, we are slowly leaving behind the condition of modernity that gradually unfolded from the 16th century onwards; second, we are moving toward the new condition of (postmodern) globality; and, third, we have not yet reached it. Indeed, like 'modernization' and other verbal nouns that end in the suffix '-ization', the term 'globalization' suggests a sort of dynamism best captured by the notion of 'development' or 'unfolding' along discernible patterns. Such unfolding may occur quickly or slowly, but it always corresponds to the idea of change, and, therefore, denotes the transformation of present conditions.

Hence, scholars who explore the dynamics of globalization are particularly keen on pursuing research questions related to the theme of social change. How does globalization occur? What is driving globalization? Is it one cause or a combination of factors? Is globalization a uniform or an uneven process? Is globalization extending modernity or is it a radical break? How does globalization differ from previous social developments? Does globalization create new forms of inequality and hierarchy? Notice that the conceptualization of globalization as an ongoing process rather than as a static condition forces the researcher to pay close attention to shifting perceptions of time and space. This explains why globalization scholars assign particular significance to historical analysis and the reconfiguration of social space.

To argue that globalization refers to a set of social processes propelling us towards the condition of globality may eliminate the danger of circular definitions, but it gives us only one defining characteristic of the process: movement towards greater interdependence and integration. Such a general definition of globalization tells us very little about its remaining qualities. In order to overcome this deficiency, we must identify additional qualities that make globalization different from other sets of social processes. Yet, whenever researchers raise the level of specificity in order to bring the phenomenon in question into sharper focus, they also heighten the danger of provoking scholarly disagreements over definitions. Our subject is no exception. One of the reasons why globalization remains a contested concept is because there exists no scholarly consensus on what kinds of social processes constitute its essence.

Despite such strong differences of opinion, however, it is possible to detect some thematic overlap in various scholarly attempts to identify the essential qualities of globalization processes. Consider, for example, the following five influential definitions of globalization. They suggest that four distinct qualities or characteristics lie at the core of the phenomenon. First, globalization involves the *creation* of new and the *multiplication* of existing social networks and activities that increasingly overcome traditional political, economic, cultural, and geographical boundaries. As we have seen in the case of Al-Jazeera television, the creation of today's satellite news corporations is made possible by the combination of professional networking, technological innovation, and political decisions that permit the emergence of new social orders that transcend parochial arrangements.

Globalization can thus be defined as the intensification of worldwide social relations which link distant localities in such a way that local happenings are shaped by events occurring many miles away and vice versa.

Anthony Giddens, Director of the London School of Economics

The concept of globalization reflects the sense of an immense enlargement of world communication, as well as of the horizon of a world market, both of which seem far more tangible and immediate than in earlier stages of modernity.

Fredric Jameson, Professor of Literature at Duke University

Globalization may be thought of as a process (or set of processes) which embodies a transformation in the spatial organization of social relations and transactions – assessed in terms of their extensity, intensity, velocity and impact – generating transcontinental or interregional flows and networks of activity, interaction, and the exercise of power.

David Held, Professor of Political Science at the
London School of Economics

Globalization as a concept refers both to the compression of the world and the intensification of consciousness of the world as a whole.

Roland Robertson, Professor of Sociology at the
University of Pittsburgh

Globalization compresses the time and space aspects of social relations.

James Mittelman, Professor of International Relations
at American University

The second quality of globalization is reflected in the *expansion* and the *stretching* of social relations, activities, and interdependencies. Today's financial markets stretch around the globe, and electronic trading occurs around the clock. Gigantic shopping malls have emerged on all continents, offering those consumers who can afford it commodities from all regions of the world – including products whose various components were manufactured in different countries. To return to our initial example, we now know that the spatial reach of Osama bin Laden's organization rapidly expanded during the late 1990s. Aided by new technology and economic deregulation, terrorist cells sprang up in dozens of nations on all five continents, ultimately turning Al Qaeda into a global terrorist network capable of planning and executing attacks on a heretofore unimaginable scale. The same process of social stretching applies to less sinister associations such as non-governmental organizations, commercial enterprises, social clubs, and countless regional and global institutions and associations such as the United Nations, the European Union, the Association of South East Asian Nations, the Organization of African Unity, the Common Market of the South, Doctors Without Borders, Amnesty International, the Union of Concerned Scientists, the World Economic Forum, Microsoft, and General Motors, to name but a few.

Third, globalization involves the *intensification* and *acceleration* of social exchanges and activities. The Internet relays distant information in mere seconds, and satellites provide consumers with real-time pictures of remote events. As Anthony Giddens notes in his definition, the intensification of worldwide social relations means that local happenings are shaped by events occurring far away, and vice versa. In other words, the seemingly opposing processes of globalization and localization actually imply each other. The 'local' and the 'global' form the endpoints of a spatial continuum whose central portion is marked by the 'national' and the 'regional'.

To elaborate on this point, let us return to the example of Osama bin Laden. It is reasonable to assume that his terrorist strategy is being shaped continuously by technological breakthroughs achieved in American and Indian computer labs, as well as by political and military decisions made in Washington, DC, Brussels, and other parts of the world. At the same time, the activities of US politicians, military engineers in the United Kingdom, and Israeli secret service agents are significantly impacted by Osama bin Laden's strategy. The often-repeated phrase that 'globalization compresses time and space' simply means that things are getting faster and distances are shrinking dramatically. As the Spanish sociologist Manuel Castells has pointed out, the current rise of the global 'network society' would not have been possible without a technological revolution – one that has been powered chiefly by the rapid development of new information and transportation technologies. Proceeding at an ever-accelerating pace, these innovations are reshaping the social landscape of human life.

Fourth, the creation, expansion, and intensification of social interconnections and interdependencies do not occur merely on an objective, material level. As Roland Robertson notes in his definition, globalization processes also involve the subjective plane of human consciousness. Hence, we must not forget that globalization also refers to people becoming increasingly conscious of growing manifestations of social interdependence and the enormous acceleration of social interactions. Their awareness of the receding importance of geographical boundaries and distances fosters a keen sense of becoming part of a global whole. Reinforced on a daily basis, these persistent experiences of global interdependence gradually change people's individual and collective identities, and thus dramatically impact the way they act in the world.

It seems that we have now identified some of the essential qualities of globalization. This allows us to offer the following definition:

> Globalization refers to a multidimensional set of social pro-
> cesses that create, multiply, stretch, and intensify worldwide
> social interdependencies and exchanges while at the same
> time fostering in people a growing awareness of deepening
> connections between the local and the distant.

More areas of contestation

Although we arrived at an adequate working definition of
globalization by drawing out some common insights that appear in
other influential definitions, we must not lose sight of the fact that
there still remain several areas of contestation. After all,
globalization is an uneven process, meaning that people living in
various parts of the world are affected very differently by this
gigantic transformation of social structures and cultural zones.
Hence, the social processes that make up globalization have been
analysed and explained by various commentators in different, often
contradictory ways. Scholars not only hold different views with
regard to proper definitions of globalization, they also disagree on
its scale, causation, chronology, impact, trajectories, and policy
outcomes. For example, the academic dispute over the scale of
globalization revolves around the question of whether it should be
understood in singular or differentiated terms. This notion of
'multidimensionality' appears as an important attribute of
globalization in our own definition; still it requires further
elaboration. The ancient Buddhist parable of the blind scholars and
their encounter with the elephant helps to illustrate the nature of
the academic controversy over the various dimensions of
globalization.

Since the blind scholars did not know what the elephant looked like,
they resolved to obtain a mental picture, and thus the knowledge
they desired, by touching the animal. Feeling its trunk, one blind
man argued that the elephant was like a lively snake. Another man,

rubbing along its enormous leg, likened the animal to a rough column of massive proportions. The third person took hold of its tail and insisted that the elephant resembled a large, flexible brush. The fourth man felt its sharp tusks and declared it to be like a great spear. Each of the blind scholars held firmly to his own idea of what constituted an elephant. Since their scholarly reputation was riding on the veracity of their respective findings, the blind men eventually ended up arguing over the true nature of the elephant.

The ongoing academic quarrel over which dimension contains the essence of globalization represents a postmodern version of the parable of the blind men and the elephant. Even those scholars who agree that globalization is best thought of as a singular process clash with each other over which aspect of social life constitutes the primary domain of the phenomenon. Some scholars argue that economic processes lie at the core of globalization. Others privilege political, cultural, or ideological aspects. Still others point to environmental processes as the essence of globalization. Like the blind men in the parable, each globalization researcher is partly right by correctly identifying *one* important dimension of the phenomenon in question. However, their collective mistake lies in their dogmatic attempts to reduce such a complex phenomenon as globalization to a single domain that corresponds to their own expertise.

To be sure, one of the central tasks for globalization researchers consists of devising better ways for gauging the relative importance of each dimension without losing sight of the interconnected whole. But it would be a grave mistake to cling to a one-sided understanding of globalization. Fortunately, more and more researchers have begun to heed this call for a genuine multidimensional approach to globalization that avoids pernicious reductionism. Since globalization contains multifaceted and differentiated processes, it is safe to say that virtually no areas of social life escape its reach. Or is it?

2. The globalization scholars and the elephant.

Before we come to this important conclusion, let us consider several objections raised by those scholars who belong to the camp of the 'globalization sceptics'. These objections range from the accusation that fashionable 'globalization talk' amounts to little more than 'globaloney' to less radical suggestions that globalization is a much more limited and uneven process than the sweeping arguments of the so-called 'hyperglobalizers' would have us believe. In many ways, the most radical globalization sceptics resemble the blind scholar who, occupying the empty space between the elephant's front and hind legs, groped in vain for a part of the elephant. Finding none, he accused his colleagues of making up fantastic stories about non-existent things, asserting that there were no such animals as 'elephants' at all.

However, evidence pointing to the rapid intensification of worldwide social relations is mounting. Hence, I will not attempt to refute those few globalization sceptics who go so far as to deny its existence altogether. On the other hand, I am rather sympathetic to the notion that globalization may be a geographically limited and uneven process. As I will argue myself in subsequent chapters, large segments of the world population – particularly in the global

South – do not enjoy equal access to thickening global networks and infrastructures. In that sense, then, globalization is associated with inequality. Nevertheless, even if it can be shown that the intensification of social interconnections and interdependencies appears to be concentrated in the economically advanced countries of the global North, it would still be entirely justified to engage in extensive 'globalization talk'. After all, the existence of patterns of rising interdependence in the global North does reflect a partial globalization trend, one that is likely to have significant impacts on other regions of the world.

In my view, the most challenging question that has emerged from the camp of globalization sceptics is the following: is globalization primarily a phenomenon of the modern age? Critics would respond to this question in the negative, adding that the concept of globalization has been applied in an historically imprecise manner. In a nutshell, this thoughtful group of sceptics contends that even a cursory look at history suggests that there is not much that is 'new' about contemporary globalization. Hence, before we explore in some detail the five main dimensions of globalization in subsequent chapters of this book, I suggest we give this weighty argument a fair hearing. Indeed, such a critical investigation of globalization's alleged novelty is closely related to yet another difficult question hotly debated in the fledgling field of globalization studies. What does a proper chronology and periodization of globalization look like? Let us turn to Chapter 2 to find answers to this question.

Chapter 2
Is globalization a new phenomenon?

If we asked an ordinary person on the streets of London, New York, Bangkok, or Rio de Janeiro about the essence of globalization, the answer would probably involve some reference to growing forms of political and economic interdependence fuelled by 'new technologies' like personal computers, the Internet, cellular phones, pagers, fax machines, palm pilots, digital cameras, high-definition televisions, satellites, jet planes, space shuttles, and supertankers. As subsequent chapters will show, however, technology provides only a partial explanation for the existence of contemporary forms of globalization. Yet, it would be foolish to deny that these new innovations have played a crucial role in the creation, multiplication, expansion, and intensification of global social interconnections and exchanges. The Internet, in particular, has assumed a pivotal function in facilitating globalization through the creation of the World Wide Web that connects billions of individuals, private associations, and governments. Since most of these technologies have been around for less than three decades, it seems to make sense to agree with those commentators who claim that globalization is, indeed, a new phenomenon.

At the same time, however, the definition of globalization we arrived at in the previous chapter stresses the dynamic nature of the phenomenon. The enhancement of worldwide interdependence and the general growth of awareness of deepening global connections are gradual processes with deep historical roots. For example, the engineers who developed laptop computers and supersonic jet planes stand on the shoulders of earlier innovators who created the steam engine, the cotton gin, the telegraph, the phonograph, the telephone, the typewriter, the internal-combustion engine, and electrical appliances. These products, in turn, owe their existence to much earlier technological inventions such as the telescope, the compass, water wheels, windmills, gunpowder, the printing press, and oceangoing ships. In order to acknowledge the full historical record, we reach back even further to such momentous technological and social achievements as the production of paper, the development of writing, the invention of the wheel, the domestication of wild plants and animals, the emergence of language, and, finally, the slow outward migration of our African ancestors at the dawn of human evolution.

Thus, the answer to the question of whether globalization constitutes a new phenomenon depends upon how far we are willing to extend the chain of causation that resulted in those recent technologies and social arrangements that most people have come to associate with this fashionable buzzword. Some scholars consciously limit the historical scope of globalization to the last four decades of postindustrialism in order to capture its contemporary features. Others are willing to extend this timeframe to include the ground-breaking developments of the 19th century. Still others argue that globalization really represents the continuation and extension of complex processes that began with the emergence of modernity and the capitalist world system some five centuries ago. And a few remaining researchers refuse to confine globalization to time periods measured in mere decades or centuries. Rather, they suggest that these processes have been unfolding for millennia.

No doubt, each of these contending perspectives contains

important insights. As we will see in subsequent chapters, the advocates of the first approach have marshalled impressive evidence for their view that the dramatic expansion and acceleration of global exchanges since the early 1970s represents a quantum leap in the history of globalization. The proponents of the second view correctly emphasize the tight connection between contemporary forms of globalization and the explosion of technology known as the Industrial Revolution. The representatives of the third perspective rightly point to the significance of the time-space compression that occurred in the 16th century. Finally, the advocates of the fourth approach advance a rather sensible argument when they insist that any truly comprehensive account of globalization falls woefully short without the incorporation of ancient developments and enduring dynamics into our planetary history.

While the short chronology outlined below is necessarily fragmentary and general, it nonetheless gives us a good sense that globalization is as old as humanity itself. This brief historical sketch identifies five distinct historical periods that are separated from each other by significant accelerations in the pace of social exchanges as well as a widening of their geographical scope. In this context, it is important to bear in mind that my chronology does not necessarily imply a linear unfolding of history, nor does it advocate a conventional Eurocentric perspective of world history. Full of unanticipated surprises, violent twists, sudden punctuations, and dramatic reversals, the history of globalization has involved all major regions and cultures of our planet.

Thus, it behoves us to refrain from imposing deterministic ideas of 'inevitability' and 'irreversibility' on globalization. However, it is important to note the occurrence of dramatic technological and social leaps in history that have pushed the intensity and global reach of these processes to new levels. Approaching our short chronology of globalization with these caveats in mind, we will be able to appreciate both the novelty of each period and the continuity of the phenomenon itself.

The prehistoric period (10,000 BCE–3,500 BCE)

Let us begin our brief historical sketch of globalization about 12,000 years ago when small bands of hunters and gatherers reached the southern tip of South America. This event marked the end of the long process of settling all five continents that was begun by our hominid African ancestors more than one million years ago. Although some major island groups in the Pacific and the Atlantic were not inhabited until relatively recent times, the truly global dispersion of our species was finally achieved. The successful endeavour of the South American nomads rested on the migratory achievements of their Siberian ancestors who had crossed the Bering Strait into North America a thousand years earlier.

In this earliest phase of globalization, contact among thousands of hunter and gatherer bands spread all over the world was geographically limited and mostly coincidental. This fleeting mode of social interaction changed dramatically about 10,000 years ago when humans took the crucial step of producing their own food. As a result of several factors, including the natural occurrence of plants and animals suitable for domestication as well as continental differences in area and total population size, only certain regions located on or near the vast Eurasian landmass proved to be ideal for these growing agricultural settlements. These areas were located in the Fertile Crescent, north-central China, North Africa, northwestern India, and New Guinea. Over time, food surpluses achieved by these early farmers and herders led to population increases, the establishment of permanent villages, and the construction of fortified towns.

Roving bands of nomads lost out to settled tribes, chiefdoms, and, ultimately, powerful states based on agricultural food production. The decentralized, egalitarian nature of hunter and gatherer groups

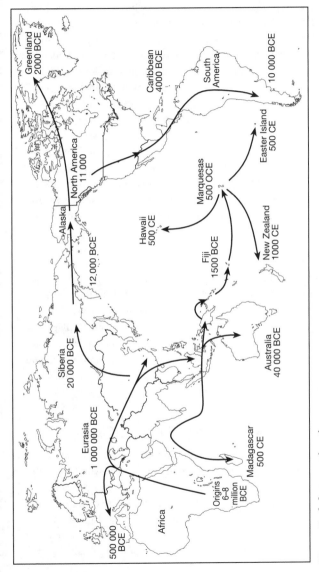

Map 1. Early human migrations.

was replaced by centralized and highly stratified patriarchal social structures headed by chiefs and priests who were exempted from hard manual labour. Moreover, for the first time in human history, these farming societies were able to support two additional social classes whose members did not participate in food production. One group consisted of full-time craft specialists who directed their creative energies toward the invention of new technologies, such as powerful iron tools and beautiful ornaments made of precious metals, complex irrigation canals, sophisticated pottery and basketry, and monumental building structures. The other group was comprised of professional bureaucrats and soldiers who would later play a key role in the monopolization of the means of violence in the hands of the rulers, the precise accounting of food surpluses necessary for the growth and survival of the centralized state, the acquisition of new territory, the establishment of permanent trade routes, and the systematic exploration of distant regions.

For the most part, however, globalization in the prehistoric period was severely limited. Advanced forms of technology capable of overcoming existing geographical and social obstacles were largely absent; thus, enduring long-distance interactions never materialized. It was only towards the end of this epoch that centrally administered forms of agriculture, religion, bureaucracy, and warfare slowly emerged as the key agents of intensifying modes of social exchange that would involve a growing number of societies in many regions of the world.

The premodern period (3,500 BCE–1,500 CE)

The invention of writing in Mesopotamia, Egypt, and central China between 3,500 and 2,000 BCE roughly coincided with the invention of the wheel around 3,000 BCE in Southwest Asia. Marking the close of the prehistoric period, these monumental inventions amounted to one of those technological and social boosts that moved globalization to a new level. Thanks to the auspicious east-west orientation of Eurasia's major continental axis – a geographical feature that had already facilitated the rapid spread of crops and animals suitable for food production along the same latitudes – the diffusion of these new technologies to distant parts of the continent occurred within only a few centuries. The importance of these inventions for the strengthening of globalization processes should be obvious. Among other things, the wheel spurred crucial infrastructural innovations such as animal-drawn carts and permanent roads that allowed for the faster and more efficient transportation of people and goods. In addition to the spread of ideas and inventions, writing greatly facilitated the coordination of complex social activities and thus encouraged large state formations. Of the sizeable territorial units that arose during this period, only the Andes civilizations of South America managed to grow into the mighty Inca Empire without the benefits of either the wheel or the written word.

3. **Assyrian clay tablet with cuneiform writing, *c.* 1900–1800** BCE.

Thus the premodern period was the age of empires. As some states succeeded in establishing permanent rule over other states, the resulting vast territorial accumulations formed the basis of the Egyptian Kingdoms, the Persian Empire, the Macedonian Empire, the American Empires of the Aztecs and the Incas, the Roman Empire, the Indian Empires, the Byzantine Empire, the Islamic Caliphates, the Holy Roman Empire, the African Empires of Ghana, Mali, and Songhay, and the Ottoman Empire. All of these empires fostered the multiplication and extension of long-distance communication and the exchange of culture, technology, commodities, and diseases. The most enduring and technologically advanced of these vast premodern conglomerates was undoubtedly the Chinese Empire. A closer look at its history reveals some of the early dynamics of globalization.

After centuries of warfare between several independent states, the Qin Emperor's armies, in 221 BCE, finally unified large portions of northeast China. For the next 1,700 years, successive dynasties known as the Han, Sui, T'ang, Yuan, and Ming ruled an empire supported by vast bureaucracies that would extend its influence to such distant regions as tropical Southeast Asia, the Mediterranean, India, and East Africa. Dazzling artistry and brilliant philosophical achievements stimulated new discoveries in other fields of knowledge such as astronomy, mathematics, and chemistry. The long list of major technological innovations achieved in China during the premodern period include redesigned plowshares, hydraulic engineering, gunpowder, the tapping of natural gas, the compass, mechanical clocks, paper, printing, lavishly embroidered silk fabrics, and sophisticated metalworking techniques. The construction of vast irrigation systems consisting of hundreds of small canals enhanced the region's agricultural productivity while at the same time providing for one of the best river transport systems in the world. The codification of law and the fixing of weights, measures, and values of coinage fostered the expansion of trade and markets. The standardization of the size of cart axles and the roads they travelled on allowed Chinese merchants for the first time to make precise calculations as to the desired quantities of imported and exported goods.

The most extensive of these trade routes was the Silk Road. It linked the Chinese and the Roman Empires, with Parthian traders serving as skilled intermediaries. Even 1,300 years after the Silk Road first reached the Italian peninsula, in 50 BCE, a truly multicultural group of Eurasian and African globetrotters – including the famous Moroccan merchant Ibn Battuta and his Venetian counterparts in the Marco Polo family – relied on this great Eurasian land route to reach the splendid imperial court of the Mongol Khans in Beijing.

By the 15th century CE, enormous Chinese fleets consisting of hundreds of 400-foot-long ocean-going ships were crossing the Indian Ocean and establishing short-lived trade outposts on the east coast of Africa. However, a few decades later, the rulers of the

4. The Great Wall of China, begun in 214 BCE and rebuilt repeatedly. The only human artefact discernible from space.

Chinese Empire implemented a series of fateful political decisions that halted overseas navigation and mandated a retreat from further technological development. Thus, they cut short their empire's incipient industrial revolution, a development that allowed much smaller European states to emerge as the primary historical agents behind the intensification of globalization.

Towards the end of the premodern period, then, the existing global trade network consisted of several interlocking trade circuits that connected the most populous regions of Eurasia and northeastern Africa. Although both the Australian and the American continents still remained separate from this expanding web of economic, political, and cultural interdependence, the empires of the Aztecs and Incas had also succeeded in developing major trade networks in their own hemisphere.

The existence of these sprawling networks of economic and cultural exchange triggered massive waves of migration, which, in turn, led to further population increase and the rapid growth of urban centres. In the resulting cultural clashes, religions with only local significance were transformed into the major 'world religions' we know today as Judaism, Christianity, Islam, Hinduism, and Buddhism. But higher population density and more intense social interaction over greater distances also facilitated the spread of new infectious diseases like the bubonic plague. The enormous plague epidemic of the mid-14th century, for example, killed up to one-third of the respective populations of China, the Middle East, and Europe. However, these unwelcome by-products of unfolding globalization processes did not reach their most horrific manifestation until the fateful 16th-century collision of the 'old' and 'new' worlds, when the nasty germs of European invaders killed an estimated 18 million Native Americans.

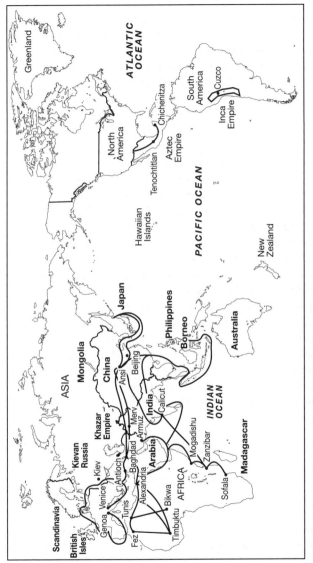

Map 2. Major world trade networks, 1000–1450.

The early modern period (1500–1750)

The term 'modernity' has become associated with the 18th-century European Enlightenment project of developing objective science, achieving a universal form of morality and law, and liberating rational modes of thought and social organization from the perceived irrationalities of myth, religion, and political tyranny. The label 'early modern', then, refers to the period between the Enlightenment and the Renaissance. During these two centuries, Europe and its social practices served as the primary catalyst for globalization. Having contributed little to technology and other civilizational achievements before about 1,000 CE, Europeans northwest of the Alps greatly benefited from the diffusion of technological innovations originating in Islamic and Chinese cultural spheres. Despite the weakened political influence of China and the noticeable ecological decline of the Fertile Crescent some 500 years later, European powers failed to penetrate into the interior of Africa and Asia. Instead, they turned their expansionistic desires westward, searching for a new, profitable sea route to India. Their efforts were aided by such innovations as mechanized printing, sophisticated wind and water mills, extensive postal systems, revised maritime technologies, and advanced navigation techniques. Add the enormous impact of the Reformation and the related liberal political idea of limited government, and we have identified the main forces behind the qualitative leap that greatly intensified demographic, cultural, ecological, and economic flows between Europe, Africa, and the Americas.

Of course, the rise of European metropolitan centres and their affiliated merchant classes represented another important factor responsible for strengthening globalization tendencies during the early modern period. Embodying the new values of individualism and unlimited material accumulation, European economic entrepreneurs laid the foundation of what later scholars would call the 'capitalist world system'. However, these fledgling capitalists could not have achieved the global expansion of their commercial enterprises without substantial support from their respective governments. The monarchs of Spain, Portugal, the Netherlands, France, and England all put significant resources into the exploration of new worlds and the construction of new interregional markets that benefited them much more than their exotic 'trading partners'. By the early 1600s, national joint stock companies like the Dutch and British East India companies were founded for the express purpose of setting up profitable overseas trade posts. As these innovative corporations grew in size and stature, they acquired the power to regulate most intercontinental economic transactions, in the process implementing social institutions and cultural practices that enabled later colonial governments to place these foreign regions under direct political rule. Related developments, such as the Atlantic slave trade and forced population transfers within the Americas, resulted in the suffering and death of millions of non-Europeans while greatly benefiting white immigrants and their home countries.

To be sure, religious warfare within Europe also created its share of dislocation and displacement for Caucasian populations. Moreover, as a result of these protracted armed conflicts, military alliances and political arrangements underwent continuous modification. Ultimately evolving from the Westphalian states system, the sovereign, territorial nation-state had emerged by 1648 as the modern container of social life. As the early modern period drew to a close, interdependencies among nation-states were multiplying as well as increasing in density.

The modern period (1750–1970)

By the late 18th century, Australia and the Pacific islands were slowly incorporated into the European-dominated network of political, economic, and cultural exchange. Increasingly

5. The sale of the island of Manhattan in 1626.

confronted with stories of the 'distant' and images of countless 'others', Europeans and their descendants on other continents took it upon themselves to assume the role of the world's guardians of universal law and morality. In spite of their persistent claims to civilizational leadership, however, they remained strangely oblivious to their racist practices and the appalling conditions of inequality that existed both within their own societies and between the West and the 'rest'. Fed by a steady stream of materials and resources that originated mostly in other regions of the world, Western capitalist enterprises gained in stature. Daring to resist powerful governmental controls, economic entrepreneurs and their academic counterparts began to spread a philosophy of individualism and rational self-interest that glorified the virtues of an idealized capitalist system supposedly based upon the providential workings of the free market and its 'invisible hand'.

Written in 1847 by the German political radicals Karl Marx and Friedrich Engels, the following passage from their famous *Communist Manifesto* captures the qualitative shift in social relations that pushed globalization to a new level in the modern period.

Indeed, the volume of world trade increased dramatically between 1850 and 1914. Guided by the activities of multinational banks,

> The discovery of America prepared the way for mighty industry and its creation of a truly global market. The latter greatly expanded trade, navigation, and communication by land. These developments, in turn, caused the further expansion of industry. The growth of industry, trade, navigation, and railroads also went hand in hand with the rise of the

> bourgeoisie and capital which pushed to the background
> the old social classes of the Middle Ages ... Chased around
> the globe by its burning desire for ever-expanding markets
> for its products, the bourgeoisie has no choice but settle
> everywhere; cultivate everywhere; establish connections
> everywhere ... Rapidly improving the instruments of
> production, the bourgeoisie utilizes the incessantly easing
> modes of communication to pull all nations into civiliza-
> tion – even the most barbarian ones ... In a nutshell, it
> creates the world in its own image.
>
> Translated by the author

capital and goods flowed across the borders relatively freely as the
sterling-based gold standard made possible the worldwide
circulation of leading national currencies like the British pound and
the Dutch gilder. Eager to acquire their own independent resource
bases, most European nation-states subjected large portions of the
global South to direct colonial rule. On the eve of World War I,
merchandise trade measured as a percentage of gross national
output totalled almost 12% for the industrialized countries, a level
unmatched until the 1970s. Global pricing systems facilitated trade
in important commodities like grains, cotton, and various metals.
Brand name packaged goods like Coca-Cola drinks, Campbell
soups, Singer sewing machines, and Remington typewriters
made their first appearance. In order to raise the global visibility of
these corporations, international advertising agencies launched
the first full-blown transborder commercial promotion
campaigns.

As Marx and Engels noted, however, the rise of the European
bourgeoisie and the related intensification of global
interconnections would not have been possible without the 19th-
century explosion of science and technology. To be sure, the

maintenance of these new industrial regimes required new power sources such as electricity and petroleum. The largely unregulated use of these energy sources resulted in the annihilation of countless animal and plant species as well as the toxification of entire regions. On the up side, however, railways, mechanized shipping, and 20th-century intercontinental air transport managed to overcome the last remaining geographical obstacles to the establishment of a genuine global infrastructure, while at the same time lowering transportation costs.

These innovations in transportation were complemented by the swift development of communication technologies. The telegraph and its transatlantic reach after 1866 provided for instant information exchanges between the two hemispheres. Moreover, the telegraph set the stage for the telephone and wireless radio communication, prompting newly emerging communication corporations like AT&T to coin advertising slogans in celebration of a world 'inextricably bound together'. Finally, the 20th-century arrival of mass circulation newspapers and magazines, film, and television further enhanced a growing consciousness of a rapidly shrinking world.

The modern period also witnessed an unprecedented population explosion. Having increased only modestly from about 300 million at the time of the birth of Christ to 760 million in 1750, the world's population reached 3.7 billion in 1970. Enormous waves of migration intensified existing cultural exchanges and transformed traditional social patterns. Popular immigration countries like the United States of America, Canada, and Australia took advantage of this boost in productivity. By the early 20th century, these countries entered the world stage as forces to be reckoned with. At the same time, however, they made significant efforts to control these large migratory flows, in the process inventing novel forms of bureaucratic control and developing new surveillance techniques designed to accumulate more information about nationals while keeping 'undesirables' out.

6. Eastern European immigrants arriving in New York City in the late 1800s.

When the accelerating process of industrialization sharpened existing disparities in wealth and well-being beyond bearable limits, many working people in the global North began to organize themselves politically in various labour movements and socialist parties. However, their idealistic calls for international class solidarity went largely unheeded. Instead, nationalist ideologies captured the imagination of millions of people around the world. There is no question that interstate rivalries intensified at the outset of the 20th century as a result of mass migration, urbanization, colonial competition, and the excessive liberalization of world trade. The ensuing period of extreme nationalism culminated in two devastating world wars, a long global economic depression, and hostile measures to protect narrowly conceived political communities.

The defeat of the axis powers in 1945 and the process of decolonization slowly revived global flows and international exchanges. A new political order of nation-states anchored in the charter of the United Nations raised the prospect of global democratic governance. During the 1950s, however, such cosmopolitan hopes quickly faded as the Cold War divided the world for four long decades into two antagonistic spheres: a liberal-capitalist camp dominated by the United States, and an authoritarian-socialist realm controlled by the Soviet Union. For the first time in human history, the spectre of a global conflict capable of destroying virtually all life on our planet had been raised.

The contemporary period (from 1970)

As we noted at the beginning of this chapter, the dramatic creation, expansion, and acceleration of worldwide interdependencies and global exchanges that have occurred since the early 1970s represent yet another quantum leap in the history of globalization. But what exactly is happening? Why does what is happening justify the creation of a buzzword that has not only captured the public imagination, but has also elicited such powerful conflicting emotional responses? Is contemporary globalization a 'good' or a 'bad' thing? Throughout this book we will consider possible answers to these crucial questions. In doing so, we will limit the application of the term 'globalization' to the contemporary period while keeping in mind that the dynamic driving these processes actually started thousands of years ago.

Before we embark on this next stage of our journey, let us pause and recall an important point we made in Chapter 1. Globalization is not a single process but a set of processes that operate simultaneously and unevenly on several levels and in various dimensions. We could compare these interactions and interdependencies to an intricate tapestry of overlapping shapes and colours. Yet, just as an auto mechanic apprentice must turn off and disassemble the car engine in order to understand its operation, so must the student of globalization apply analytical distinctions in order to make sense of the web of global interdependencies. In ensuing chapters we will identify, explore, and assess patterns of globalization in each domain while keeping in mind its operation as an interacting whole. Although we will study the various dimensions of globalization in isolation, we will resist the temptation to reduce globalization to a single aspect. Thus will we avoid the blunder that kept the blind men from appreciating the multidimensional nature of the elephant.

Chapter 3
The economic dimension of globalization

At the beginning of the previous chapter we noted that new forms of technology are one of the hallmarks of contemporary globalization. Indeed, technological progress of the magnitude seen in the last three decades is a good indicator for the occurrence of profound social transformations. Changes in the way in which people undertake economic production and organize the exchange of commodities represent one obvious aspect of the great transformation of our age. Economic globalization refers to the intensification and stretching of economic interrelations across the globe. Gigantic flows of capital and technology have stimulated trade in goods and services. Markets have extended their reach around the world, in the process creating new linkages among national economies. Huge transnational corporations, powerful international economic institutions, and large regional trading systems have emerged as the major building blocs of the 21st century's global economic order.

The emergence of the global economic order

Contemporary economic globalization can be traced back to the gradual emergence of a new international economic order assembled at an economic conference held towards the end of World War II in the sleepy New England town of Bretton Woods. Under the leadership of the United States of America and Great

Britain, the major economic powers of the global North reversed their protectionist policies of the interwar period (1918–39). In addition to arriving at a firm commitment to expand international trade, the participants of the conference also agreed to establish binding rules on international economic activities. Moreover, they resolved to create a more stable money exchange system in which the value of each country's currency was pegged to a fixed gold value of the US dollar. Within these prescribed limits, individual nations were free to control the permeability of their borders. This allowed states to set their own political and economic agendas.

Bretton Woods also set the institutional foundations for the establishment of three new international economic organizations. The International Monetary Fund was created to administer the international monetary system. The International Bank for Reconstruction and Development, later known as the World Bank, was initially designed to provide loans for Europe's postwar reconstruction. During the 1950s, however, its purpose was expanded to fund various industrial projects in developing countries around the world. Finally, the General Agreement on Tariffs and Trade was established in 1947 as a global trade organization charged with fashioning and enforcing multilateral trade agreements. In 1995, the World Trade Organization was founded as the successor organization to GATT. As we will see in Chapter 8, the WTO became, in the 1990s, the focal point of intense public controversy over the design and the effects of economic globalization.

In operation for almost three decades, the Bretton Woods regime contributed greatly to the establishment of what some observers have called the 'golden age of controlled capitalism'. Existing mechanisms of state control over international capital movements made possible full employment and the expansion of the welfare state. Rising wages and increased social services secured in the

7. The Bretton Woods Conference of 1944.

wealthy countries of the global North a temporary class compromise. By the early 1970s, however, the Bretton Woods system collapsed. Its demise strengthened those integrationist economic tendencies that later commentators would identify as the birth pangs of the new global economic order. What happened?

In response to profound political changes in the world that were undermining the economic competitiveness of US-based industries, President Richard Nixon abandoned the gold-based fixed rate system in 1971. The ensuing decade was characterized by global economic instability in the form of high inflation, low economic growth, high unemployment, public sector deficits, and two unprecedented energy crises due to OPEC's ability to control a large part of the world's oil supply. Political forces in the global North most closely identified with the model of controlled capitalism suffered a series of spectacular election defeats at the hands of conservative political parties who advocated a 'neoliberal' approach to economic and social policy.

Neoliberalism

Neoliberalism is rooted in the classical liberal ideals of Adam Smith (1723–90) and David Ricardo (1772–1823), both of whom viewed the market as a self-regulating mechanism tending toward equilibrium of supply and demand, thus securing the most efficient allocation of resources. These British philosophers considered that any constraint on free competition would interfere with the natural efficiency of market mechanisms, inevitably leading to social stagnation, political corruption, and the creation of unresponsive state bureaucracies. They also advocated the elimination of tariffs on imports and other barriers to trade and capital flows between nations. British sociologist Herbert Spencer (1820–1903) added to this doctrine a twist of social Darwinism by arguing that free market economies constitute the most civilized form of human competition in which the 'fittest' would naturally rise to the top.

Yet, in the decades following World War II, even the most conservative political parties in Europe and the United States rejected those *laissez-faire* ideas and instead embraced a rather extensive version of state interventionism propagated by British economist John Maynard Keynes, the architect of the Bretton Woods system. By the 1980s, however, British Prime Minister Margaret Thatcher and US President Ronald Reagan led the neoliberal revolution against Keynesianism, consciously linking the notion of globalization to the 'liberation' of economies around the world.

This new neoliberal economic order received further legitimation with the 1989–91 collapse of communism in the Soviet Union and Eastern Europe. Since then, the three most significant

Concrete neoliberal measures include:

1. Privatization of public enterprises
2. Deregulation of the economy
3. Liberalization of trade and industry
4. Massive tax cuts
5. 'Monetarist' measures to keep inflation in check, even at the risk of increasing unemployment
6. Strict control on organized labour
7. The reduction of public expenditures, particularly social spending
8. The down-sizing of government
9. The expansion of international markets
10. The removal of controls on global financial flows

developments related to economic globalization have been the internationalization of trade and finance, the increasing power of transnational corporations, and the enhanced role of international economic institutions like the IMF, the World Bank, and the WTO. Let us briefly examine these important features.

The internationalization of trade and finance

Many people associate economic globalization with the controversial issue of free trade. After all, the total value of world trade exploded from $57 billion in 1947 to an astonishing $6 trillion in the late 1990s. In the last few years, the public debate over the alleged benefits and drawbacks of free trade reached a feverish pitch as wealthy Northern countries have increased their efforts to establish a single global market through regional and international trade-liberalization agreements such NAFTA and GATT. Free trade proponents assure the public that the elimination or reduction of existing trade barriers among nations will enhance consumer choice, increase global wealth, secure peaceful international relations, and spread new technologies around the world.

To be sure, there is evidence that some national economies have increased their productivity as a result of free trade. Moreover, there are some benefits that accrue to societies through specialization, competition, and the spread of technology. But it is less clear whether the profits resulting from free trade have been distributed fairly within and among countries. Most studies show that the gap between rich and poor countries is widening at a fast pace. Hence, free trade proponents have encountered severe criticism from labour unions and environmental groups who claim that the elimination of social control mechanisms has resulted in a lowering of global labour standards, severe forms of ecological degradation, and the growing indebtedness of the global South to the North. We will return to the issue of global inequality in Chapter 7.

The internationalization of trade has gone hand in hand with the liberalization of financial transactions. Its key components include the deregulation of interest rates, the removal of credit controls, and the privatization of government-owned banks and financial institutions. Globalization of financial trading allows for increased mobility among different segments of the financial industry, with fewer restrictions and greater investment opportunities. This new financial infrastructure emerged in the 1980s with the gradual deregulation of capital and securities markets in Europe, the Americas, East Asia, Australia, and New Zealand. A decade later, Southeast Asian countries, India, and several African nations followed suit.

During the 1990s, new satellite systems and fibre-optic cables provided the nervous system of Internet-based technologies that further accelerated the liberalization of financial transactions. As captured by the snazzy title of Microsoft CEO Bill Gates'

The global South: a fate worse than debt

Amount of money owed by the world's 47 poorest and most indebted nations	$422 billion
Amount of money spent by Western industrialized nations on weapons and soldiers every year	$422 billion
Amount of money raised by 'Live Aid' in 1985 to combat famine in Ethiopia	$200 million
Amount of money all African countries need for weekly foreign debt service (interest only)	$200 million
Amount of money the United Nations estimates is needed annually to curb the AIDS epidemic in Africa through education, prevention, and care	$15 billion
Amount of money African nations pay to service their debts each year (interest only)	$13.5 billion
Annual income per person in Zaire	$110
Amount of money each resident of Zaire would have to pay to extinguish the country's debt to foreign creditors	$236
Percent of the Zambian budget allocated for foreign debt repayment in 1997	40%
Percent of the Zambian budget allocated for basic social services, including healthcare and education	7%
Percent of debt owed by the world's most heavily indebted nations that the World Bank and IMF can afford to cancel without jeopardizing their operations	100%
Percent of debt that they have actually agreed to cancel	33%
Profits made by Exxon in 2000	16.9 billion

Total debt burden of Benin, Burundi, Chad, Guinea Bissau, Sao Tome, Togo, Rwanda, Central African Republic, Sierra Leone, Mali, Somalia, and Niger	16.9 billion

Sources: David Roodman, *Still Waiting for the Jubilee: Pragmatic Solutions to the Third World Debt Crisis*, Worldwatch paper 1555 (Washington, DC: Worldwatch Institute, April 2001): Jubilee 2000 United Kingdom website www.jubilee2000uk.org, viewed 17 May 2001; Jubilee U.S.A. Network website www.j2000usa.org/action5.htm; Drop the Debt website www.dropthedebt.org, viewed 22 May 2001; Joseph Kahn, 'U.S. offers Africa billions to fight AIDS', *New York Times*, 18 July 2000. Secondary Source: World Watch, Vol. 14, No. 4, July/August 2001, p. 39.

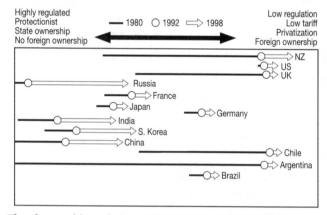

The advance of deregulation and liberalization, 1980–98.

Source: Vincent Cable, *Globalization and Global Governance* (The Royal Institute of International Affairs, 1999), p. 20.

best-selling book, many people conducted *business@the-speed-of-thought*. Millions of individual investors utilized global electronic investment networks not only to place their orders, but also to receive valuable information about relevant economic and political developments. In 2000, 'e-businesses', 'dot.com firms', and other virtual participants in the information-based 'new economy' traded about 400 billion dollars over the Web in the United States alone. In 2003, global business-to-business transactions are projected to reach 6 trillion dollars. Ventures that will connect the stock exchanges in New York, London, Frankfurt, and Tokyo are at the advanced planning stage. Such a financial 'supermarket' in cyberspace would span the entire globe, stretching its electronic tentacles into countless decentralized investment networks that relay billions of trades at breathtaking velocities.

Yet, a large part of the money involved in these global financial exchanges has little to do with supplying capital for such productive investments as putting together machines or organizing raw materials and employees to produce saleable commodities. Most of the financial growth has occurred in the form of high-risk 'hedge funds' and other purely money-dealing currency and securities markets that trade claims to draw profits from future production. In other words, investors are betting on commodities or currency rates that do not yet exist. For example, in 2000, the equivalent of over 2 trillion US dollars was exchanged daily in global currency markets alone. Dominated by highly sensitive stock markets that drive high-risk innovation, the world's financial systems are characterized by high volatility, rampant competition, and general insecurity. Global speculators often take advantage of weak financial and banking regulations to make astronomical profits in emerging markets of developing countries. However, since these international capital flows can be reversed swiftly, they are capable of creating artificial boom-and-bust cycles that endanger the social welfare of entire regions. The 1997–8 Southeast Asia Crisis represents but one of these recent economic reversals brought on by the globalization of financial transactions.

8. The New York Stock Exchange. Billions of shares change hands on an average trading day.

The Southeast Asia Crisis

In the 1990s, the governments of Thailand, Indonesia, Malaysia, South Korea, and the Philippines gradually abandoned control over the domestic movement of capital in order to attract foreign direct investment. Intent on creating a stable money environment, they raised domestic interest rates and linked their national currencies to the value of the US dollar. The ensuing irrational euphoria of international investors translated into soaring stock and real estate markets all over Southeast Asia. However, by 1997, those investors realized that prices had become inflated much beyond their actual value. They panicked and withdrew a total of $105 billion from these countries, forcing governments in the region to abandon the dollar peg. Unable to halt the ensuing free fall of their currencies, those governments used up their entire foreign exchange reserves. As a result, economic output fell, unemployment increased, and wages plummeted. Foreign banks and creditors reacted by declining new credit applications and refusing to extend existing loans. By late 1997, the entire region found itself in the throes of a financial crisis that threatened to push the global economy into recession. This disastrous result was only narrowly averted by a combination of international bail-out packages and the immediate sale of Southeast Asian commercial assets to foreign corporate investors at rock-bottom prices. Today, ordinary citizens in Southeast Asia are still suffering from the devastating social and political consequences of that economic meltdown.

The power of transnational corporations

Transnational corporations are the contemporary versions of
the early modern commercial enterprises we discussed in the
previous chapter. Powerful firms with subsidiaries in several
countries, their numbers skyrocketed from 7,000 in 1970 to about
50,000 in 2000. Enterprises like General Motors, Walmart,
Exxon-Mobil, Mitsubishi, and Siemens belong to the 200
largest TNCs, which account for over half of the world's industrial
output. None of these corporations maintains headquarters outside
of North America, Europe, Japan, and South Korea. This
geographical concentration reflects existing asymmetrical power
relations between the North and the South. Yet, clear power
differentials can also be found within the global North. In 1999, 142
of the leading 200 TNCs were based in only three countries – the
United States, Japan, and Germany.

Rivalling nation-states in their economic power, these corporations
control much of the world's investment capital, technology, and
access to international markets. In order to maintain their
prominent positions in the global marketplace, TNCs frequently
merge with other corporations. Some of these recent mergers
include the $160-billion marriage of the world's largest Internet
provider, AOL, with entertainment giant Time-Warner; the
purchase of Chrysler Motors by Daimler-Benz for $43 billion; and
the $115-billion merger between Sprint Corporation and MCI
WorldCom. A close look at corporate sales and country GDPs
reveals that 51 of the world's 100 largest economies are
corporations; only 49 are countries. Hence, it is not surprising
that some critics have characterized economic globalization as
'corporate globalization' or 'globalization-from-above'.

TNCs have consolidated their global operations in an increasingly
deregulated global labour market. The availability of cheap labour,
resources, and favourable production conditions in the global South
has enhanced corporate mobility and profitability. Accounting for

Transnational corporations versus countries: a comparison

	Country	GDP ($ mil)	Corporation	Sales ($ mil)
1.	Denmark	174,363.0	General Motors	176,558.0
2.	Poland	154,146.0	Wal-Mart	166,809.0
3.	South Africa	131,127.0	Exxon Mobil	163,881.0
4.	Israel	99,068.0	Royal Dutch/ Shell	105,366.0
5.	Ireland	84,861.0	IBM	87,548.0
6.	Malaysia	74,634.0	Siemens	75,337.0
7.	Chile	71,092.0	Hitachi	71,858.5
8.	Pakistan	59,880.0	Sony	60,052.7
9.	New Zealand	53,622.0	Honda Motor	54,773.5
10.	Hungary	48,355.0	Credit Suisse	49,362.0

Sources: Sales: *Fortune*, 31 July 2000; GDP: World Bank, *World Development Report 2000*.

over 70% of world trade, TNCs have boosted their foreign direct investments by approximately 15% annually during the 1990s. Their ability to disperse manufacturing processes into many discrete phases carried out in many different locations around the world reflects the changing nature of global production. Such transnational production networks allow TNCs like Nike, General Motors, and Volkswagen to produce, distribute, and market their products on a global scale. Nike, for example, subcontracts 100% of its goods production to 75,000 workers in China, South Korea, Malaysia, Taiwan, and Thailand. Transnational production networks augment the power of global capitalism by making it easier for TNCs to bypass nationally based trade unions and other workers' organizations. Anti-sweatshop activists around the world have responded to these tactics by enlisting public participation in several successful consumer boycotts and other forms of nonviolent direct action.

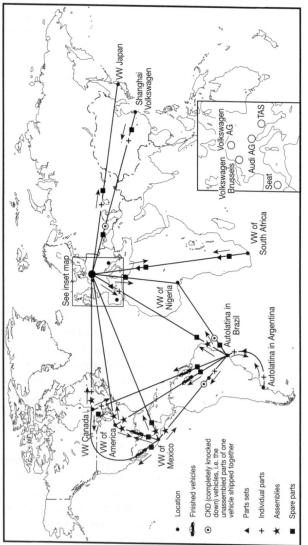

Map 3. Volkswagen's transnational production network.

No doubt, the growing power of TNCs has profoundly altered the structure and functioning of the international economy. These giant firms and their global strategies have become major determinants of trade flows, the location of industries, and other economic activities around the world. As a consequence, TNCs have become extremely important players that influence the economic, political, and social welfare of many nations. Here is a final example.

Nokia's role in the Finnish economy

Named after a small town in southwest Finland, Nokia Corporation rose from modest beginnings a little more than a decade ago to become a large TNC that manufactures 37 of every 100 cellphones sold worldwide. Today, its products connect one billion people in an invisible web around the globe. However, Nokia's gift to Finland – the distinction of being the most interconnected nation in the world – came at the price of economic dependency. Nokia is the engine of Finland's economy, representing two-thirds of the stock market's value and one-fifth of the nation's total export. It employs 22,000 Finns, not counting the estimated 20,000 domestic employees who work for companies that depend on Nokia contracts. The corporation produces a large part of Finland's tax revenue, and its \$25 billion in annual sales almost equals the entire national budget. Yet, when Nokia's growth rate slowed in recent years, company executives let it be known that they were dissatisfied with the country's relatively steep income tax. Today, many Finnish citizens fear that decisions made by relatively few Nokia managers might pressure the government to lower corporate taxes and abandon the country's generous and egalitarian welfare system.

The enhanced role of international economic institutions

The three international economic institutions most frequently mentioned in the context of economic globalization are the IMF, the World Bank, and the WTO. These three institutions enjoy the privileged position of making and enforcing the rules of a global economy that is sustained by significant power differentials between the global North and South. Since we will discuss the WTO in some detail in Chapters 7 and 8, let us focus here on the other two institutions. As pointed out above, the IMF and the World Bank emerged from the Bretton Woods system. During the Cold War, their important function of providing loans for developing countries became connected to the West's political objective of containing communism. Starting in the 1970s, and especially after the fall of the Soviet Union, the economic agenda of the IMF and the World Bank has synchronized neoliberal interests to integrate and deregulate markets around the world.

In return for supplying much-needed loans to developing countries, the IMF and the World Bank demand from their creditor nations the implementation of so-called 'structural adjustment programmes'. Unleashed on developing countries in the 1990s, this set of neoliberal policies is often referred to as the 'Washington Consensus'. It was devised and codified by John Williamson, who was an IMF adviser in the 1970s. The various sections of the programme were mainly directed at countries with large foreign debts remaining from the 1970s and 1980s. The official purpose of the document was to reform the internal economic mechanisms of debtor countries in the developing world so that they would be in a better position to repay the debts they had incurred. In practice, however, the terms of the programme spelled out a new form of colonialism. The ten points of the Washington Consensus, as defined by Williamson, required governments to implement the following structural adjustments in order to qualify for loans:

1. A guarantee of fiscal discipline, and a curb to budget deficits;
2. A reduction of public expenditure, particularly in the military and public administration;
3. Tax reform, aiming at the creation of a system with a broad base and with effective enforcement;
4. Financial liberalization, with interest rates determined by the market;
5. Competitive exchange rates, to assist export-led growth;
6. Trade liberalization, coupled with the abolition of import licensing and a reduction of tariffs;
7. Promotion of foreign direct investment;
8. Privatization of state enterprises, leading to efficient management and improved performance;
9. Deregulation of the economy;
10. Protection of property rights.

It is no coincidence that this programme is called the 'Washington Consensus', for, from the outset, the United States has been the dominant power in the IMF and the World Bank. Unfortunately, however, large portions of the 'development loans' granted by these institutions have either been pocketed by authoritarian political leaders or have enriched local businesses and the Northern corporations they usually serve. Sometimes, exorbitant sums are spent on ill-considered construction projects. Most importantly, however, structural adjustment programmes rarely produce the desired result of 'developing' debtor societies, because mandated cuts in public spending translate into fewer social programmes, reduced educational opportunities, more environmental pollution, and greater poverty for the vast majority of people. Typically, the largest share of the national budget is spent on servicing outstanding debts. For example, in 1997, developing countries paid a combined $292 billion in debt service, while receiving only $269 billion in new loans. This means that the net transfer of wealth from the global South to the North was $23 billion. Pressured by antiglobalist forces, the IMF and the World Bank were only recently willing to consider a new policy of blanket debt forgiveness in special cases.

Neoliberal economics and Argentina

Less than a decade ago, IMF and World Bank officials held up Argentina as a 'model developing country'. Having accepted substantial structural adjustment programmes that led to the privatization of state enterprises, the reduction of tariffs, and the elimination of many social programmes, the Argentine government celebrated low unemployment rates, a stable currency pegged to the dollar, and strong foreign investment. For a few short years, neoliberal economics seemed vindicated. However, as the IMF demanded even stronger austerity measures in return for new loans, the Argentine economy went sour. In June 2000, the country was paralysed by mass strikes against the government's new austerity package designed to meet IMF deficit guidelines and thus retain access to the Fund's $7.2 billion emergency line of credit. In January 2002, after months of violent street protests in major cities, Argentina formally defaulted on its massive public debt of $141 billion. In order to prevent the complete financial and social collapse of his nation, Eduardo Duhalde, the country's fifth president in only two weeks, further limited people's access to their savings deposits and decoupled the peso from the dollar. Within hours, the currency lost a third of its value, robbing ordinary people of the fruits of their labour. 'Argentina is broke, sunk,' the President admitted, 'and this [neoliberal] model has swept everything away with it.'

As this chapter has shown, economic perspectives on globalization can hardly be discussed apart from an analysis of political process and institutions. After all, the intensification of global economic interconnections does not simply fall from the sky; rather, it is set into motion by a series of political decisions. Hence, while acknowledging the importance of economics in our story of globalization, this chapter nonetheless ends with the suggestion that we ought to be sceptical of one-sided accounts that identify expanding economic activity as both the primary aspect of globalization and the engine behind its rapid development. The multidimensional nature of globalization demands that we flesh out in more detail the interaction between its political and economic aspects.

Chapter 4
The political dimension of globalization

Political globalization refers to the intensification and expansion of political interrelations across the globe. These processes raise an important set of political issues pertaining to the principle of state sovereignty, the growing impact of intergovernmental organizations, and the future prospects for regional and global governance. Obviously, these themes respond to the evolution of political arrangements beyond the framework of the nation-state, thus breaking new conceptual ground. After all, for the last few centuries, humans have organized their political differences along territorial lines that generate a sense of 'belonging' to a particular nation-state.

This artificial division of planetary social space into 'domestic' and 'foreign' spheres corresponds to people's collective identities based on the creation of a common 'us' and an unfamiliar 'them'. Thus, the modern nation-state system has rested on psychological foundations and cultural assumptions that convey a sense of existential security and historical continuity, while at the same time demanding from its citizens that they put their national loyalties to the ultimate test. Nurtured by demonizing images of the Other, people's belief in the superiority of their own nation has supplied the mental energy required for large-scale warfare – just as the enormous productive capacities of the modern state have provided the material means necessary to fight the 'total wars' of the last century.

Contemporary manifestations of globalization have led to the partial permeation of these old territorial borders, in the process also softening hard conceptual boundaries and cultural lines of demarcation. Emphasizing these tendencies, commentators belonging to the camp of hyperglobalizers have suggested that the period since the late 1960s has been marked by a radical 'deterritorialization' of politics, rule, and governance. Considering such pronouncements premature at best and erroneous at worst, globalization sceptics have not only affirmed the continued relevance of the nation-state as the political container of modern social life but have also pointed to the emergence of regional blocs as evidence for new forms of territorialization. As each group presents different assessments of the fate of the modern nation-state, they also quarrel over the relative importance of political and economic factors.

Out of these disagreements there have emerged three fundamental questions that probe the extent of political globalization. First, is it really true that the power of the nation-state has been curtailed by massive flows of capital, people, and technology across territorial boundaries? Second, are the primary causes of these flows to be found in politics or in economics? Third, are we witnessing the emergence of global governance? Before we respond to these questions in more detail, let us briefly consider the main features of the modern nation-state system.

The modern nation-state system

The origins of the modern nation-state system can be traced back to 17th-century political developments in Europe. In 1648, the Peace of Westphalia concluded a series of religious wars among the main European powers following the Protestant Reformation. Based on the newly formulated principles of sovereignty and territoriality, the ensuing model of self-contained, impersonal states challenged the medieval mosaic of small polities in which political power tended to be local and personal in focus but still subordinated to a larger imperial authority. While the emergence of the Westphalian model did not eclipse the transnational character of vast imperial domains overnight, it nonetheless gradually strengthened a new conception of international law based on the principle that all states had an equal right to self-determination. Whether ruled by absolutist kings in France and Prussia or in a more democratic fashion by the constitutional monarchs and republican leaders of England and the Netherlands, these unified territorial areas constituted the foundation for modernity's secular and national system of political power. According to political scientist David Held, the Westphalian model contained the following essential points:

1. The world consists of, and is divided into, sovereign territorial states which recognize no superior authority.

2. The processes of law-making, the settlement of disputes, and law enforcement are largely in the hands of individual states.

3. International law is oriented to the establishment of minimal rules of co-existence; the creation of enduring relationships is an aim, but only to the extent that it allows state objectives to be met.

4. Responsibility for cross-border wrongful acts is a 'private matter' concerning only those affected.

5. All states are regarded as equal before the law, but legal rules do not take account of asymmetries of power.

6. Differences among states are often settled by force; the principle of effective power holds sway. Virtually no legal fetters exist to curb the resort to force; international legal standards afford only minimal protection.

7. The collective priority of all states should be to minimize the impediments to state freedom.

The centuries following the Peace of Westphalia saw the further centralization of political power, the expansion of state administration, the development of professional diplomacy, and the successful monopolization of the means of coercion in the hands of the state. Moreover, states also provided the military means required for the expansion of commerce, which, in turn, contributed to the spread of this European form of political rule around the globe.

The modern nation-state system found its mature expression at the end of World War I in US President Woodrow Wilson's famous 'Fourteen Points' based on the principle of national self-determination. But his assumption that all forms of national identity should be given their territorial expression in a sovereign 'nation-state' proved to be extremely difficult to enforce in practice. Moreover, by enshrining the nation-state as the ethical and legal pinnacle of his proposed interstate system, Wilson unwittingly lent some legitimacy to those radical ethnonationalist forces that pushed the world's main powers into another war of global proportions.

Yet, Wilson's commitment to the nation-state coexisted with his internationalist dream of establishing a global system of collective security under the auspices of a new international organization, the League of Nations. His idea of giving international cooperation an institutional expression was eventually realized with the founding of the United Nations in 1945. While deeply rooted in a political order based on the modern nation-state system, the UN and other fledgling intergovernmental organizations also served as catalysts for the gradual extension of political activities across national boundaries, thus undermining the principle of national sovereignty.

As globalization tendencies grew stronger during the 1970s, it

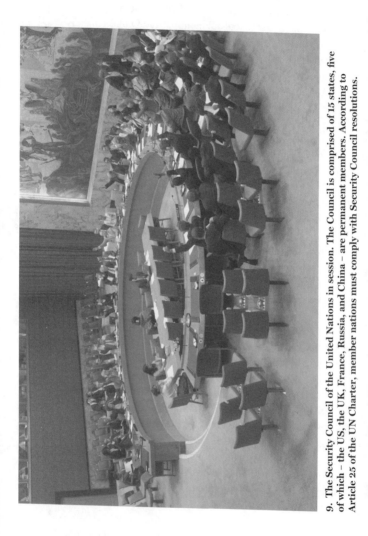

9. The Security Council of the United Nations in session. The Council is comprised of 15 states, five of which – the US, the UK, France, Russia, and China – are permanent members. According to Article 25 of the UN Charter, member nations must comply with Security Council resolutions.

became clear that the international society of separate states was rapidly turning into a global web of political interdependencies that challenged the sovereignty of nation-states. In 1990, at the outset of the Gulf War, US President George H. W. Bush effectively pronounced dead the Westphalian model by announcing the birth of a 'new world order' whose leaders no longer respected the idea that cross-border wrongful acts were a matter concerning only those states affected. Did this mean that the modern nation-state system was no longer viable?

The demise of the nation-state?

Hyperglobalizers respond to the above question affirmatively. At the same time, most of them consider political globalization a mere secondary phenomenon driven by more fundamental economic and technological forces. They argue that politics has been rendered almost powerless by an unstoppable techno-economic juggernaut that will crush all governmental attempts to reintroduce restrictive policies and regulations. Endowing economics with an inner logic apart from, and superior to, politics, these commentators look forward to a new phase in world history in which the main role of government will be to serve as a superconductor for global capitalism.

Pronouncing the rise of a 'borderless world', hyperglobalizers seek to convince the public that globalization inevitably involves the decline of bounded territory as a meaningful concept for understanding political and social change. Consequently, this group of commentators suggests that political power is located in global social formations and expressed through global networks rather than through territorially based states. In fact, they argue that nation-states have already lost their dominant role in the global economy. As territorial divisions are becoming increasingly irrelevant, states are even less capable of determining the direction of social life within their borders. For example, since the workings of genuinely global capital markets dwarf their ability to control exchange rates or protect their currency, nation-states have become vulnerable to the discipline imposed by economic choices made elsewhere, over which states have no practical control. Hyperglobalizers insist that the minimalist political order of the future will be determined by regional economies linked together in an almost seamless global web of production and exchange.

A group of globalization sceptics disagrees, highlighting instead the central role of politics in unleashing the forces of globalization, especially through the successful mobilization of political power. In their view, the rapid expansion of global economic activity can be reduced neither to a natural law of the market nor to the development of computer technology. Rather, it originated with political decisions to lift international restrictions on capital made by neoliberal governments in the 1980s and 1990s. Once those decisions were implemented, global markets and new technologies came into their own. The clear implication of this perspective is that territory still matters. Hence, globalization sceptics insist on the continued relevance of conventional political units, operating either in the form of modern nation-states or global cities.

In my view, the arguments of both hyperglobalizers and sceptics remain entangled in a particularly vexing version of the chicken-and-the-egg problem. After all, economic forms of interdependence are set into motion by political decisions, but these decisions are nonetheless made in particular economic contexts. As we have noted in previous chapters, the economic and political aspects of globalization are profoundly interconnected. There is no question that recent economic developments such as trade liberalization and deregulation have significantly constrained the set of political options open to states, particularly in the global South. For example, it has become much easier for capital to escape taxation and other national policy restrictions. Thus, global markets frequently undermine the capacity of governments to set independent national policy objectives and impose their own domestic standards. Hence, we ought to acknowledge the decline of the nation-state as a sovereign entity and the ensuing devolution of state power to regional and local governments as well as to various supranational institutions.

On the other hand, such a concession does not necessarily mean that nation-states have become impotent bystanders to the workings of global forces. Governments can still take measures to make their economies more or less attractive to global investors. In addition, nation-states have retained control over education, infrastructure, and, most importantly, population movements. Indeed, immigration control, together with population registration and monitoring, has often been cited as the most notable exception to the general trend towards global integration. Although only 2% of the world's population live outside their country of origin, immigration control has become a central issue in most advanced nations. Many governments seek to restrict population flows, particularly those originating in the poor countries of the global South. Even in the United States, annual inflows of about 600,000 immigrants during the 1990s reached only half the levels recorded during the first two decades of the 20th century.

Finally, the series of drastic national security measures that were implemented worldwide as a response to the terrorist attacks of 9/11 reflect political dynamics that run counter to the hyperglobalizers' predictions of a borderless world. Some civil rights advocates even fear that the enormous resurgence of patriotism around the world might enable states to re-impose restrictions on the freedom of movement and assembly. At the same time, however, the activities of global terrorist networks have revealed the inadequacy of conventional national security structures based on the modern nation-state system, thus forcing national governments to engage in new forms of international cooperation.

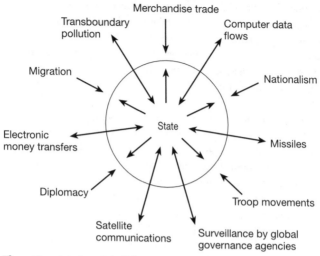

The nation-state in a globalizing world.

Source: Jan Aart Scholte, 'The globalization of world politics', in John Baylis and Steve Smith (eds.), *The Globalization of World Politics*, 2nd edn. (Oxford University Press, 2001), p. 22.

Overall, then, we ought to reject premature pronouncements of the impending demise of the nation-state while acknowledging its increasing difficulties in performing some of its traditional functions. Contemporary globalization has weakened some of the conventional boundaries between domestic and foreign policies while fostering the growth of supraterritorial social spaces and institutions that, in turn, unsettle traditional political arrangements. At the outset of the 21st century, the world finds itself in a transitional phase between the modern nation-state system and postmodern forms of global governance.

Political globalization and global governance

Political globalization is most visible in the rise of supraterritorial institutions and associations held together by common norms and interests. In this early phase of global governance, these structures resemble an eclectic network of interrelated power centres such as municipal and provincial authorities, regional blocs, international organizations, and national and international private-sector associations.

On the municipal and provincial level, there has been a remarkable growth in the number of policy initiatives and transborder links between various sub-state authorities. For example, Chinese provinces and US federal states have established permanent missions and points of contact, some of which operate relatively autonomously with little oversight from their respective national governments. Various provinces and federal states in Canada, India, and Brazil are beginning to develop their own trade agendas and financial strategies to obtain loans. An example of international cooperation on the municipal level is the rise of powerful city networks like the World Association of Major Metropolises that develop cooperative ventures to deal with common local issues across national borders. 'Global cities' like Tokyo, London, New York, and Singapore tend to be more closely connected to each other than they are to many cities in their home countries.

On the regional level, there has been an extraordinary proliferation of multilateral organizations and agreements. Regional clubs and agencies have sprung up across the world, leading some observers to speculate that they will eventually replace nation-states as the basic unit of governance. Starting out as attempts to integrate regional economies, these regional blocs have, in some cases, already evolved into loose political federations with common institutions of governance. For example, the European Community began in 1950 with French Foreign Minister Robert Schuman's modest plan to create a supranational institution charged with regulating French and German coal and steel production. Half a century later, 15 member states have formed a close community with political institutions that create common public policies and design binding security arrangements. Following the dissolution of the Soviet Union in 1991, many of the formerly communist countries in Eastern Europe have submitted their formal accession applications to the EU.

On a global level, governments have formed a number of international organizations, including the UN, NATO, WTO, and OECD. Full legal membership of these organizations is open to

Map 4. The eastward expansion of the European Union.

states only, and the decision-making authority lies with representatives from national governments. The proliferation of these transworld bodies has shown that nation-states find it increasingly difficult to manage sprawling networks of social interdependence.

Finally, the emerging structure of global governance is also shaped by 'global civil society', a realm populated by thousands of voluntary, non-governmental associations of worldwide reach. International NGOs like Amnesty International or Greenpeace represent millions of ordinary citizens who are prepared to challenge political and economic decisions made by nation-states and intergovernmental organizations. We will examine the antiglobalist activities of some of these organizations in Chapter 8.

Some globalization researchers believe that political globalization might facilitate the emergence of democratic transnational social forces anchored in this thriving sphere of global civil society. Predicting that democratic rights will ultimately become detached from their narrow relationship to discrete territorial units, these optimistic voices anticipate the creation of a democratic global

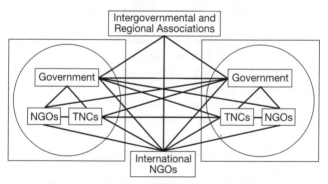

Incipient global governance: a network of interrelated power centres.

Source: adapted from Peter Willets, 'Transnational actors and international organizations in global politics', in Baylis and Smith, *The Globalization of World Politics*, p. 379.

governance structure based on Western cosmopolitan ideals, international legal arrangements, and a web of expanding linkages between various governmental and non-governmental organizations. If such a promising scenario indeed will come to pass, then the final outcome of political globalization might well be the emergence of a cosmopolitan democracy that would constitute the basis for a plurality of identities flourishing within a structure of mutual toleration and accountability. According to David Held, one of the chief proponents of this view, the cosmopolitan democracy of the future would contain the following political features:

1. A global parliament connected to regions, states, and localities;
2. A new charter of rights and duties locked into different domains of political, social, and economic power;
3. The formal separation of political and economic interests;
4. An interconnected global legal system with mechanisms of enforcement from the local to the global.

A number of less optimistic commentators have challenged the idea that political globalization is moving in the direction of cosmopolitan democracy. Most criticisms boil down to the charge that such a vision indulges in an abstract idealism that fails to engage current political developments on the level of public policy. Sceptics have also expressed the suspicion that the proponents of cosmopolitanism do not consider in sufficient detail the cultural feasibility of global democracy. In other words, the worldwide intensification of cultural, political, and economic interaction makes the possibility of resistance and opposition just as real as the benign vision of mutual accommodation and tolerance of differences. To follow up on this cultural dimension of globalization, let us turn to the next chapter.

Chapter 5
The cultural dimension of globalization

Even a very short introduction to globalization would be woefully inadequate without an examination of its cultural dimension. Cultural globalization refers to the intensification and expansion of cultural flows across the globe. Obviously, 'culture' is a very broad concept; it is frequently used to describe the whole of human experience. In order to avoid the ensuing problem of overgeneralization, it is important to make analytical distinctions between aspects of social life. For example, we associate the adjective 'economic' with the production, exchange, and consumption of commodities. If we are discussing the 'political', we mean practices related to the generation and distribution of power in societies. If we are talking about the 'cultural', we are concerned with the symbolic construction, articulation, and dissemination of meaning. Given that language, music, and images constitute the major forms of symbolic expression, they assume special significance in the sphere of culture.

The exploding network of cultural interconnections and interdependencies in the last decades has led some commentators to suggest that cultural practices lie at the very heart of contemporary globalization. Yet, cultural globalization did not start with the worldwide dissemination of rock 'n' roll, Coca-Cola, or football. As noted in Chapter 2, expansive civilizational exchanges are much older than modernity. Still, the volume and extent of cultural transmissions in the contemporary period have far exceeded those of earlier eras. Facilitated by the Internet and other new technologies, the dominant symbolic systems of meaning of our age – such as individualism, consumerism, and various religious discourses – circulate more freely and widely than ever before. As images and ideas can be more easily and rapidly transmitted from one place to another, they profoundly impact the way people experience their everyday lives. Today, cultural practices frequently escape fixed localities such as town and nation, eventually acquiring new meanings in interaction with dominant global themes.

The thematic landscape traversed by scholars of cultural globalization is vast and the questions they raise are too numerous to be fleshed out in this short introduction. Rather than offering a long laundry list of relevant topics, this chapter will focus on four important themes: the tension between sameness and difference in the emerging global culture; the crucial role of transnational media corporations in disseminating popular culture; the globalization of languages; and the impact of materialist and consumerist values on our planet's ecological systems.

Global culture: sameness or difference?

Does globalization make people around the world more alike or more different? This is the question most frequently raised in discussions on the subject of cultural globalization. A group of commentators we might call 'pessimistic hyperglobalizers' argue in favour of the former. They suggest that we are not moving towards a cultural rainbow that reflects the diversity of the world's existing cultures. Rather, we are witnessing the rise of an increasingly homogenized popular culture underwritten by a Western 'culture industry' based in New York, Hollywood, London, and Milan. As evidence for their interpretation, these commentators point to Amazonian Indians wearing Nike training shoes, denizens of the Southern Sahara purchasing Texaco baseball caps, and Palestinian youths proudly displaying their Chicago Bulls sweatshirts in downtown Ramallah. Referring to the diffusion of Anglo-American values and consumer goods as the 'Americanization of the world', the proponents of this cultural homogenization thesis argue that Western norms and lifestyles are overwhelming more vulnerable cultures. Although there have been serious attempts by some countries to resist these forces of 'cultural imperialism' – for example, a ban on satellite dishes in Iran, and the French imposition of tariffs and quotas on imported film and television – the spread of American popular culture seems to be unstoppable.

But these manifestations of sameness are also evident inside the dominant countries of the global North. American sociologist George Ritzer coined the term 'McDonaldization' to describe the wide-ranging sociocultural processes by which the principles of the fast-food restaurant are coming to dominate more and more sectors of American society as well as the rest of the world. On the surface, these principles appear to be rational in their attempts to offer efficient and predictable ways of serving people's needs. However, looking behind the façade of repetitive TV commercials that claim to 'love to see you smile', we can identify a number of serious problems. For one, the generally low nutritional value of fast-food meals – and particularly their high fat content – has been implicated in the rise of serious health problems such as heart disease, diabetes, cancer, and juvenile obesity. Moreover, the impersonal, routine operations of 'rational' fast-service establishments actually undermine expressions of forms of cultural diversity. In the long run, the McDonaldization of the world amounts to the imposition of uniform standards that eclipse human creativity and dehumanize social relations.

Perhaps the most thoughtful analyst in this group of pessimistic hyperglobalizers is American political theorist Benjamin Barber. In his popular book on the subject, he warns his readers against the

Number of types of packaged bread available at a Safeway in Lake Ridge, Virginia	104
Number of those breads containing no hydrogenated fat or diglycerides	0
Amount of money spent by the fast food industry on television advertising per year	$3 billion
Amount of money spent promoting the National Cancer Institute's 'Five A Day' programme, which encourages the consumption of fruits and vegetables to prevent cancer and other diseases	$1 million
Number of 'coffee drinks' available at Starbucks, whose stores accommodate a stream of over 5 million customers per week, most of whom hurry in and out	26
Number of 'coffee drinks' in the 1950s coffee houses of Greenwich Village, New York City	2
Number of new models of cars available to suburban residents in 2001	197
Number of convenient alternatives to the car available to most such residents	0
Number of US daily newspapers in 2000	1,483
Number of companies that control the majority of those newspapers	6
Number of leisure hours the average American has per week	35
Number of hours the average American spends watching television per week	28

Sources: Eric Schossler, *Fast Food Nation* (Houghton & Mifflin, 2001), p. 47; www.naa.org/info/facts00/11.htm; *Consumer Reports Buying Guide 2001* (Consumers Union, 2001), pp. 147–163; Laurie Garrett, *Betrayal of Trust* (Hyperion, 2000), p. 353; www.roper.com/news/content/news169.htm; *The World Almanac and Book of Facts 2001* (World Almanac Books, 2001), p. 315; www.starbucks.com.

cultural imperialism of what he calls 'McWorld' – a soulless consumer capitalism that is rapidly transforming the world's diverse populations into a blandly uniform market. For Barber, McWorld is a product of a superficial American popular culture assembled in the 1950s and 1960s, driven by expansionist commercial interests. Music, video, theatre, books, and theme parks are all constructed as American image exports that create common tastes around common logos, advertising slogans, stars, songs, brand names, jingles, and trademarks.

Barber's insightful account of cultural globalization also contains the important recognition that the colonizing tendencies of McWorld provoke cultural and political resistance in the form of 'Jihad' – the parochial impulse to reject and repel the homogenizing forces of the West wherever they can be found. As we noted in our deconstruction of Osama bin Laden in Chapter 1, Jihad draws on the furies of religious fundamentalism and ethnonationalism which constitute the dark side of cultural particularism. Fuelled by opposing universal aspirations, Jihad and McWorld are locked in a bitter cultural struggle for popular allegiance. Barber asserts that both forces ultimately work against a participatory form of democracy, for they are equally prone to undermine civil liberties and thus thwart the possibility of a global democratic future.

Optimistic hyperglobalizers agree with their pessimistic colleagues that cultural globalization generates more sameness, but they consider this outcome to be a good thing. For example, American social theorist Francis Fukuyama explicitly welcomes the global spread of Anglo-American values and lifestyles, equating the Americanization of the world with the expansion of democracy and free markets. But optimistic hyperglobalizers do not just come in the form of American chauvinists who apply the old theme of manifest destiny to the global arena. Some representatives of this camp consider themselves staunch cosmopolitans who celebrate the Internet as the harbinger of a homogenized 'techno-culture'. Others

10. Jihad vs McWorld: selling fast food in Indonesia.

are free-market enthusiasts who embrace the values of global consumer capitalism.

It is one thing to acknowledge the existence of powerful homogenizing tendencies in the world, but it is quite another to assert that the cultural diversity existing on our planet is destined to vanish. In fact, several influential commentators offer a contrary assessment that links globalization to new forms of cultural expression. Sociologist Roland Robertson, for example, contends that global cultural flows often reinvigorate local cultural niches. Hence, rather than being totally obliterated by the Western consumerist forces of sameness, local difference and particularity still play an important role in creating unique cultural constellations. Arguing that cultural globalization always takes place in local contexts, Robertson rejects the cultural homogenization thesis and speaks instead of 'glocalization' – a complex interaction of the global and local characterized by cultural borrowing. The resulting expressions of cultural 'hybridity' cannot be reduced to clear-cut manifestations of 'sameness' or 'difference'. As we noted in our previous discussion of Osama bin Laden, such processes of hybridization have become most visible in fashion, music, dance, film, food, and language.

In my view, the respective arguments of hyperglobalizers and sceptics are not necessarily incompatible. The contemporary experience of living and acting across cultural borders means both the loss of traditional meanings and the creation of new symbolic expressions. Reconstructed feelings of belonging coexist in uneasy tension with a sense of placelessness. Cultural globalization has contributed to a remarkable shift in people's consciousness. In fact, it appears that the old structures of modernity are slowly giving way to a new 'postmodern' framework characterized by a less stable sense of identity and knowledge.

Given the complexity of global cultural flows, one would actually expect to see uneven and contradictory effects. In certain contexts, these flows might change traditional manifestations of national identity in the direction of a popular culture characterized by sameness; in others they might foster new expressions of cultural particularism; in still others they might encourage forms of cultural hybridity. Those commentators who summarily denounce the homogenizing effects of Americanization must not forget that hardly any society in the world today possesses an 'authentic', self-contained culture. Those who despair at the flourishing of cultural hybridity ought to listen to exciting Indian rock songs, admire the intricacy of Hawaiian pidgin, or enjoy the culinary delights of Cuban-Chinese cuisine. Finally, those who applaud the spread of consumerist capitalism need to pay attention to its negative consequences, such as the dramatic decline of communal sentiments as well as the commodification of society and nature.

The role of the media

To a large extent, the global cultural flows of our time are generated and directed by global media empires that rely on powerful communication technologies to spread their message. Saturating global cultural reality with formulaic TV shows and mindless advertisements, these corporations increasingly shape people's identities and the structure of desires around the world. During the last two decades, a small group of very large TNCs have come to dominate the global market for entertainment, news, television, and film. In 2000, only ten media conglomerates – AT&T, Sony, AOL/Time Warner, Bertelsmann, Liberty Media, Vivendi Universal, Viacom, General Electric, Disney, and News Corporation – accounted for more than two-thirds of the $250–275 billion in annual worldwide revenues generated by the communications industry. In the first half of that year, the volume of merger deals in global media, Internet, and telecommunications totalled $300 billion, three times the figure for the first six months of 1999.

As recently as 15 years ago, not one of the giant corporations that dominate what Benjamin Barber has appropriately called the 'infotainment telesector' existed in its present form as a media company. In 2001, nearly all of these corporations ranked among the largest 300 non-financial firms in the world. Today, most media analysts concede that the emergence of a global commercial-media market amounts to the creation of a global oligopoly similar to that of the oil and automotive industries in the early part of the 20th century. The crucial cultural innovators of earlier decades – small, independent record labels, radio stations, movie theatres, newspapers, and book publishers – have become virtually extinct as they found themselves incapable of competing with the media giants.

The negative consequences of this shotgun marriage of finance and culture are obvious. TV programmes turn into global 'gossip markets', presenting viewers and readers of all ages with the vacuous details of the private lives of American celebrities like Britney Spears, Jennifer Lopez, Leonardo DiCaprio, and Kobe Bryant. Evidence suggests that people all over the world – but especially those from wealthy countries of the Northern hemisphere – are watching more television than ever before. For example, the daily average viewing time per TV home in the United States has increased from 5 hours and 56 minutes in 1970 to 7 hours and 26 minutes in 1999. That same year, TV household penetration in the US stood at a record 98.3%, with 73.9% of TV households owning two or more sets. Advertisement clutter on US television reached unprecedented levels in 2000, peaking at over 15 minutes of commercials per prime time TV hour, not including the frequent cutaways for local ads. The TV advertisement volume in the US has increased from \$3.60 billion in 1970 to \$50.44 billion in 1999. Recent studies show that American children at age 12 watch an average of 20,000 TV commercials a year, and 2-year-old toddlers have already developed brand loyalties.

The 'Big Ten' media conglomerates in 2001

AT&T CORPORATION (partial or majority ownership of the following)

Television: 7 networks (including WB, HBO, E!), 1 production company, largest cable provider

Movies: 3 studios (including Warner Bros)

Radio: 43 stations in Canada

Music: 1 production company (Quincy Jones Entertainment Co.)

SONY (partial or majority ownership of the following)

Television: 4 networks (including Telemundo, Music Choice, Game Show Network)

Movies: 4 studios (including Columbia Pictures), 1 movie theatre chain (Loews)

Music: 4 labels (including Columbia, Epic, American), 1 recording studio (Whitfield)

AOL/TIME WARNER (partial or majority ownership of the following)

Television: 15 networks (including WB, HBO, TBS, TNT, CNN), second-largest cable provider, 4 production companies (including Warner Bros, Castle Rock), library of 6,500 movies, 32,000 TV shows, 1 digital video recording company (TiVo)

Magazines: 64 titles (including *People*, *Life*, *Time*)

Movies: 3 studios (including Warner Bros, New Line)

Music: 40 labels (including Atlantic, Elektra, Rhino), 1 production company (Quincy Jones Entertainment Co.)

Internet: 4 Internet companies (including America Online, CompuServe, Netscape), 7 websites (including MusicNet, Winamp, moviefone)

BERTELSMANN (partial or majority ownership of the following)

Television: 22 stations in Europe, Europe's biggest broadcaster

Internet: 6 websites (including Lycos, MusicNet, Get Music, barnesandnoble.com)

Magazines: 80 titles (including *YM*, *Family Circle*, *Fitness*)

Radio: 18 stations in Europe

Music: 200 labels (including Arista, RCA, BMG Classics)

Newspapers: 11 dailies in Germany and Eastern Europe

LIBERTY MEDIA CORPORATION (partial or majority ownership of the following)

Television: 20 networks (including Discovery, USA Network, Sci-Fi Channel, QVC), 14 stations, largest cable operator in Japan, 2 production companies (MacNeil/Lehrer Productions), 1 digital video recording company (TiVo)

Internet: 3 websites (including Ticketmaster, Citysearch)

Movies: 6 studios (including USA Films, Gramercy Pictures, October Films)

Radio: 21 stations in US, 49 stations in Canada

Magazines: 101 titles (including *American Baby*, *Modern Bride*, *Seventeen*)

VIVENDI UNIVERSAL (partial or majority ownership of the following)

Television: 34 channels in 15 countries (including USA Network, Sundance Channel), cable operations in 11 countries, 2 production studios (Universal Studios)

Movies: 6 studios (including Universal Studios, PolyGram Films, Gramercy Pictures)

Music: 10 labels (including Interscope, Def Jam, MCA)

Internet: 1 Internet company (Vizzavi), 2 websites (Get Music, iWON.com)

Magazines: 2 titles (*L'Express*, *L'Expansion*)

Newspapers: Free papers in France

VIACOM, INC. (partial or majority ownership of the following)

Television: 18 networks (including CBS, UPN, MTV, Nickelodeon), 39 stations, 7 production studios, 1 digital video recording company (TiVo)

Movies: 4 studios, 1 movie rental chain (Blockbuster)

Internet: 8 websites (including Sportsline.com, hollywood.com, iWON.com)

Magazines: 4 titles (including *BET Weekend*, *Emerge*, *Heart & Soul*)

Radio: 184 Infinity radio stations, CBS Radio Network

GENERAL ELECTRIC (partial or majority ownership of the following)

Television: 12 networks (including NBC, A&E, Bravo), 13 stations and PAX TV, 5 production studios, 1 digital video recording company (TiVo)

Internet: 6 websites (including Salon.com, Autobytel.com, polo.com)

WALT DISNEY COMPANY (partial or majority ownership of the following)

Television: 17 networks (including ABC, ESPN, Lifetime), 10 stations, 6 production studios (including Buena Vista, Touchstone, Saban)

Movies: 6 studios (including Dimension, Miramax Film Corp., Touchstone Pictures)

Radio: 50 stations and 4 networks

Magazines: 6 titles (including *US Weekly*, *Discover*, *Talk*)

NEWS CORPORATION (partial or majority ownership of the following)

Television: 14 networks (including Fox, National Geographic Channel, Golf Channel), 33 stations, 5 production studios (including Regency Television, XYZ Entertainment), 1 digital video recording company (TiVo)

Movies: 7 studios (including Fox Searchlight, New Regency, Twentieth Century Fox)

Music: 1 label (Rawkus)

Newspapers: 7 dailies (including *NY Post*, *The Sun*, *The Australian*)

Adapted from *The Nation*, 7/14 January 2002

The values disseminated by transnational media enterprises secure not only the undisputed cultural hegemony of popular culture, but also lead to the depoliticization of social reality and the weakening of civic bonds. One of the most glaring developments of the last two decades has been the transformation of news broadcasts and educational programmes into shallow entertainment shows. Given that news is less than half as profitable as entertainment, media firms are increasingly tempted to pursue higher profits by ignoring journalism's much vaunted separation of newsroom practices and business decisions. Partnerships and alliances between news and entertainment companies are fast becoming the norm, making it more common for publishing executives to press journalists to cooperate with their newspapers' business operations. A sustained attack on the professional autonomy of journalism is, therefore, also part of cultural globalization.

The globalization of languages

One direct method of measuring and evaluating cultural changes brought about by globalization is to study the shifting global patterns of language use. The globalization of languages can be viewed as a process by which some languages are increasingly used in international communication while others lose their prominence and even disappear for lack of speakers. Researchers at the Globalization Research Center at the University of Hawai'i have identified five key variables that influence the globalization of languages:

1. *Number of languages*: The declining number of languages in different parts of the world points to the strengthening of homogenizing cultural forces.
2. *Movements of people*: People carry their languages with them when they migrate and travel. Migration patterns affect the spread of languages.

> 3. *Foreign language learning and tourism*: Foreign language learning and tourism facilitate the spread of languages beyond national or cultural boundaries.
> 4. *Internet languages*: The Internet has become a global medium for instant communication and quick access to information. Language use on the Internet is a key factor in the analysis of the dominance and variety of languages in international communication.
> 5. *International scientific publications*: International scientific publications contain the languages of global intellectual discourse, thus critically impacting intellectual communities involved in the production, reproduction, and circulation of knowledge around the world.

The figure on p. 84 illustrates the relationships among these five variables.

Given these highly complex interactions, research in this area frequently yields contradictory conclusions. The figure above represents only one possible conceptualization of the meaning and effects of language globalization. Unable to reach a general agreement, experts in the field have developed several different hypotheses. One model posits a clear correlation between the growing global significance of a few languages – particularly English, Chinese, Spanish, and French – and the declining number of other languages around the world. Another model suggests that the globalization of language does not necessarily mean that our descendants are destined to utilize only a few tongues. Still another thesis emphasizes the power of the Anglo-American culture industry to make English *the* global lingua franca of the 21st century.

To be sure, the rising significance of the English language has a long history, reaching back to the birth of British colonialism in the late

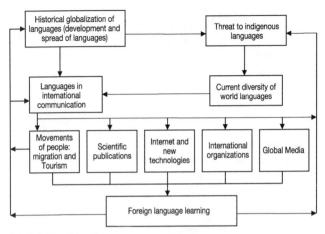

The globalization of languages.

Source: Adapted from Globalization Research Center at the University of Hawai'i-Manoa, www.globalhawaii.org.

16th century. At that time, only approximately 7 million people used English as their mother tongue. By the 1990s, this number had swollen to over 350 million native speakers, with 400 million more using English as a second language. Today, more than 80% of the content posted on the Internet is in English. Almost half of the world's growing population of foreign students are enrolled at institutions in Anglo-American countries.

At the same time, however, the number of spoken languages in the world has dropped from about 14,500 in 1500 to less than 7,000 in 2000. Given the current rate of decline, some linguists predict that 50–90% of the currently existing languages will have disappeared by the end of the 21st century.

But the world's languages are not the only entities threatened with extinction. The spread of consumerist values and materialist lifestyles has endangered the ecological health of our planet as well.

The declining number of languages around the world, 1500–2000

Continents	Early 16th century		Early 17th century		Early 18th century	
	Number	%	Number	%	Number	%
Americas	2,175	15	2,025	15	1,800	15
Africa	4,350	30	4,050	30	3,600	30
Europe	435	3	405	3	360	3
Asia	4,785	33	4,455	33	3,960	33
Pacific	2,755	19	2,565	19	2,280	19
World	14,500	100	13,500	100	12,000	100

Continents	Early 19th century		Early 20th century		Late 20th century		Early 21st century	
	Number	%	Number	%	Number	%	Number	%
Americas	1,500	15	1,125	15	1,005	15	366	12
Africa	3,000	30	2,250	30	2,011	30	1,355	45
Europe	300	3	225	3	201	3	140	5
Asia	3,300	33	2,475	33	2,212	33	1,044	38
Pacific	1,900	19	1,425	19	1,274	19	92	3
World	10,000	100	7,500	100	6,703	100	2,997	100

Source: Globalization Research Center at the University of Hawai'i-Manoa, www.globalhawaii.org.

Cultural values and environmental degradation

How people view their natural environment depends to a great
extent on their cultural milieu. For example, cultures steeped in
Taoist, Buddhist, and various animist religions tend to emphasize
the interdependence of all living beings – a perspective that calls for
a delicate balance between human wants and ecological needs.
Judeo-Christian humanism, on the other hand, contains deeply
dualistic values that put human beings at the centre of the universe.
Nature is considered a 'resource' to be used instrumentally to fulfil
human desires. The most extreme manifestation of this
anthropocentric paradigm is reflected in the dominant values and
beliefs of consumerism. As pointed out above, the US-dominated
culture industry seeks to convince its global audience that the
meaning and chief value of life can be found in the limitless
accumulation of material possessions.

At the dawn of the 21st century, however, it has become impossible
to ignore the fact that people everywhere on this planet are
inextricably linked to each other through the air they breathe, the
climate they depend upon, the food they eat, and the water they
drink. In spite of this obvious lesson of interdependence, our
planet's ecosystems are subjected to continuous human assault in
order to secure wasteful lifestyles. Granted, some of the major
ecological challenges the world faces today are problems that
afflicted civilizations even in ancient times. But until the coming of
the Industrial Revolution, environmental degradation was
relatively localized and occurred over thousands of years. In the last
few decades, the scale, speed, and depth of Earth's environmental
decline have been unprecedented. Let us briefly consider some of
the most dangerous manifestations of the globalization of
environmental degradation.

Two of the major concerns relate to uncontrolled population growth
and lavish consumption patterns in the global North. Since farming
economies first came into existence about 480 generations ago, the

Major manifestations and consequences of global environmental degradation.

Source: Author.

global population has exploded a thousand-fold to more than 6 billion. Half of this increase has occurred in the last 30 years. With the possible exception of some rodent species, humans are now the most numerous mammals on earth. Vastly increased demands for food, timber, and fibre have put severe pressure on the planet's ecosystems. Today, large areas of the Earth's surface, especially in arid and semi-arid regions, have nearly ceased to be biologically productive.

Concerns about the relationship between population growth and environmental degradation are frequently focused rather narrowly on aggregate population levels. Yet, the global impact of humans on the environment is as much a function of per capita consumption as it is of overall population size. For example, the United States comprises only 6% of the world's population, but it consumes

30–40% of our planet's natural resources. Together, regional overconsumption and uncontrolled population growth present a serious problem to the health of our planet. Unless we are willing to change the underlying cultural and religious value structure that sustains these ominous dynamics, the health of Mother Earth is likely to deteriorate even further.

Annual consumption patterns (per capita) in selected countries in 2001

Country	Meat (kg)	Paper (kg)	Fossil fuels (kg of oil equivalent)	Passenger cars (per 1,000 people)	Total value of private consumption
United States	122	293	6,902	489	$21,680
Japan	42	239	3,277	373	$15,554
Poland	73	54	2,585	209	$5,087
China	47	30	700	3.2	$1,410
Zambia	12	1.6	77	17	$625

Source: US Public Broadcasting Service, http://www.pbs.org/earthonedge/science/trends.html.

Human-induced climate change such as global warming represents another example of the decisive shift in both the intensity and extent of contemporary environmental problems. The rapid build-up of gas emissions, including carbon dioxide, methane, nitrous and sulphur oxides, and chlorofluorocarbons, in our planet's atmosphere has greatly enhanced Earth's capacity to trap heat. The resulting 'greenhouse effect' is responsible for raising average temperatures worldwide.

Although the precise effects of global warming are difficult to calculate, the US Union of Concerned Scientists has presented data suggesting that the global average temperature increased from about 13.5°C (56.3°F) in 1880 to 14.4°C (57.9°F) in 2000. Further increases in global temperatures could lead to partial meltdowns of

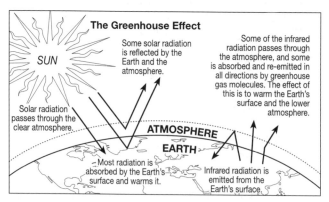

11. The Greenhouse Effect.

the polar ice caps, causing global sea levels to rise by up to 90 centimetres by 2100 – a catastrophic development that would threaten the many coastal regions around the world.

Transboundary pollution represents another grave danger to our collective survival. The release of vast amounts of synthetic chemicals into the air and water has created conditions for human and animal life that are outside previous limits of biological experience. For example, chlorofluorocarbons have been used in the second half of the 20th century as nonflammable refrigerants, industrial solvents, foaming agents, and aerosol propellants. In the mid-1970s, researchers noted that the unregulated release of CFCs into the air seemed to be depleting Earth's protective ozone layer. A decade later, the discovery of large 'ozone holes' over Tasmania, New Zealand, and large parts of the Antarctic finally resulted in a coordinated international effort to phase out production of CFCs and other ozone-depleting substances. Other forms of transboundary pollution include industrial emissions of sulphur and nitrogen oxides. Returning to the ground in the form of 'acid rain', these chemicals damage forests, soils, and freshwater ecosystems. Current acid deposits in Northern Europe and parts of North America are at least twice as high as the critical level suggested by environmental agencies.

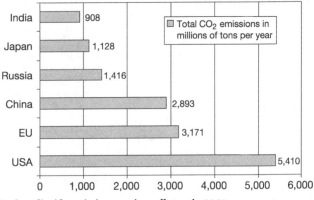

Carbon dioxide emissions: major polluters in 2001.

Source: BBC Science-Technology, http://news6.thdo.bbc.co.uk.

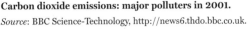

Perhaps the most ominous problem associated with globalization of environmental degradation in the contemporary era is the worldwide destruction of biodiversity. In 1998, a group of US scientists rated biodiversity loss as a more serious environmental problem than global warming or transboundary pollution. Seven out of ten biologists today believe the world is now in the midst of the fastest mass extinction of living species in the 4.5-billion-year history of the planet. According to recent OECD reports, two-thirds of the world's farmlands have been rated as 'somewhat degraded' and one-third have been marked as 'strongly degraded'. Half the world's wetlands have already been destroyed, and the biodiversity of freshwater ecosystems is under serious threat. Three-quarters of worldwide genetic diversity in agricultural crop and animal breeds has been lost since 1900. Some experts fear that up to 50% of all plant and animal species – most of them in the global South – will disappear by the end of this century.

Despite this litany of bad ecological news, one might find reason for cautious optimism in the rising number of international environmental treaties and agreements. Various clauses in these accords curtail air and water pollution, protect endangered species, and limit hazardous waste disposal. Unfortunately, however, most of these treaties lack effective international enforcement mechanisms. Moreover, such major environmental polluters as the United States and China have not yet ratified some of the key agreements.

Major global environmental treaties, 1971–2002

Name	Coverage/protection	Date
Ramsar Convention, Iran	Wetlands	1971
UNESCO-World Heritage, Paris	Cultural and natural heritage	1972
UNEP Conference, Stockholm	General environment	1972
CITES, Washington, DC	Endangered species	1973
Marine Pollution Treaty, London	Marine pollution from ships	1978
UN Convention on Law of the Sea	Marine species, pollution	1982
Vienna Protocol	Ozone layer	1985
Montreal Protocol	Ozone layer	1987
Basel Convention	Hazardous wastes	1989
UN 'Rio Summit' on Environment	Climate change, biodiversity	1992
Jakarta Mandate	Marine and coastal diversity	1995
Kyoto Protocol	Global warming	1997
Rotterdam Convention	Industrial pollution	1998
Johannesburg World Summit	Ecological sustainability, pollution	2002

Source: Author.

In 1992, the Union of Concerned Scientists issued a communiqué entitled 'Warning to Humanity', which stated that the global environment was in the throes of a severe crisis. More than 1,500 scientists, including many Nobel laureates, have signed the document. It remains to be seen whether the growing recognition of the ecological limits of our planet will translate into a much-needed revision of cultural structures rooted in the desire for the unlimited accumulation of material things.

Chapter 6
The ideological dimension of globalization

An ideology can be defined as a system of widely shared ideas, patterned beliefs, guiding norms and values, and ideals accepted as truth by a particular group of people. Ideologies offer individuals a more or less coherent picture of the world not only as it is, but also as it ought to be. In doing so, they help organize the tremendous complexity of human experience into fairly simple, but frequently distorted, images that serve as guide and compass for social and political action. These simplified and distorted ideas are often employed to legitimize certain political interests or to defend dominant power structures. Seeking to imbue society with their preferred norms and values, ideologists present the public with a circumscribed agenda of things to discuss, claims to make, and questions to ask. They speak to their audience in stories and narratives that persuade, praise, condemn, distinguish 'truths' from 'falsehoods', and separate the 'good' from the 'bad'. Thus, ideology connects theory and practice by orienting and organizing human action in accordance with generalized claims and codes of conduct.

Like all social processes, globalization contains an ideological dimension filled with a range of norms, claims, beliefs, and narratives about the phenomenon itself. For example, the heated public debate over whether globalization represents a 'good' or a 'bad' thing occurs in the arena of ideology. Hence, before exploring the ideological dimension of globalization, we should make an important analytical distinction between *globalization* – social processes of intensifying global interdependence that have been described by various commentators in different, often contradictory ways – and *globalism* – an ideology that endows the concept of globalization with neoliberal values and meanings.

As we will see in Chapter 7, various social groups have contested this association of neoliberal values with globalization, seeking instead to endow the concept with different norms and meanings. Up to now, however, the ideals expressed by these groups have not been able to dislodge the dominant neoliberal discourse of globalism. The latter is disseminated worldwide by a powerful phalanx of social forces located chiefly in the global North, consisting of corporate managers, executives of large transnational corporations, corporate lobbyists, journalists and public-relations specialists, intellectuals writing to a large public audience, state

12. **Microsoft CEO Bill Gates, one of the world's most powerful advocates of globalism.**

bureaucrats, and politicians. Serving as the chief advocates of globalism, these individuals saturate the public discourse with idealized images of a consumerist, free-market world.

Selling globalization

In 2002, the neoliberal American magazine *Business Week* featured a cover story on globalization that contained the following statement: 'For nearly a decade, political and business leaders have struggled to persuade the American public of the virtues of globalization.' Citing the results of a national poll on globalization conducted in April 2000, the article goes on to report that most Americans seem to be of two minds on the subject. On one hand, about 65% of the respondents think that globalization is a 'good thing' for consumers and businesses in both the United States and the rest of the world. On the other, they are afraid that globalization might lead to a significant loss of American jobs. In addition, nearly 70% of those polled believe that free trade agreements with low-wage countries are responsible for driving down wages in the United States. Ending on a rather combative note, the article issues a stern warning to American politicians and business leaders not to be caught off guard by the arguments of antiglobalist forces. In order to assuage people's increasing anxiety on the subject, American decision makers ought to be more effective in highlighting the benefits of globalization. After all, the persistence of public fears over globalization might result in a significant backlash, jeopardizing the health of the international economy and 'the cause of free trade'.

The cover story contains two important pieces of information with regard to the ideological dimensions of globalization. First, there is the open admission that political and business leaders are actively engaged in selling their preferred version of globalization to the public. In fact, the author of the *Business Week* article sees the construction of arguments and images that portray globalization in a positive light as an indispensable tool for the realization of a global order based on free-market principles. No doubt, such favourable visions of globalization pervade public opinion and political choices. Today, neoliberal decision makers have had to become expert designers of an attractive ideological container for their market-friendly political agenda. Given that the exchange of commodities constitutes the core activity of all market societies, the discourse of globalization itself has turned into an extremely important commodity destined for public consumption.

Second, the polling data presented in the *Business Week* cover story reveal the existence of a remarkable cognitive dissonance between people's normative orientation towards globalization and their personal experiences in the globalizing world. How can one explain that a sizeable majority of respondents is afraid of the negative economic impact of globalization on their lives while at the same time deeming globalization to be a 'good thing'? The obvious answer is ideology. Glowing neoliberal narratives of globalization have shaped a large part of public opinion around the world, even where people's daily experiences reflect a less favourable picture.

Business Week, *The Economist*, *Forbes*, the *Wall Street Journal*, and the *Financial Times* are among the most powerful of dozens of magazines, journals, newspapers, and electronic media published in the wealthy countries of the Northern Hemisphere that feed their readers a steady diet of globalist claims. Globalism has become what some social and political thinkers call a 'strong discourse' – one that is notoriously difficult to resist and repel because it has on its side powerful social forces that have already pre-selected what counts as 'real' and, therefore, shape the world accordingly. The constant repetition and public recitation of globalism's central claims and slogans have the capacity to produce what they name. As more neoliberal policies are enacted, the claims of globalism become even more firmly planted in the public mind.

In the remainder of this chapter, we will identify and analyse five major ideological claims that occur with great regularity in the utterances, speeches, and writings of influential advocates of globalism. It is important to note that globalists themselves construct these claims in order to sell their political and economic agenda. It may be true that no single globalist speech or piece of writing contains all of the five assertions discussed below, but all of them contain at least some of these claims.

Claim 1: Globalization is about the liberalization and global integration of markets

Like all ideologies, globalism starts with the attempt to establish an authoritative account of what the phenomenon is all about. For neoliberals, such a definition is anchored in the idea of the self-regulating market that serves as the framework for a future global order. As we noted in Chapter 3, neoliberals seek to cultivate in the popular mind the uncritical association of 'globalization' with what they assert to be the benefits of market liberalization. In particular, they present the liberalization and integration of global markets as 'natural' phenomena that further individual liberty and material progress in the world. Here are three examples (see p. 98).

The problem with this claim is that the globalist message of liberalizing and integrating markets is only realizable through the *political* project of engineering free markets. Thus, globalists must be prepared to utilize the *powers of government* to weaken and eliminate those social policies and institutions that curtail the market. Since only strong governments are up to this ambitious task of transforming existing social arrangements, the successful liberalization of markets depends upon *intervention* and *interference* by centralized state power. Such actions, however, stand in stark contrast to the neoliberal idealization of the limited role of government. Yet, globalists do expect governments to play an extremely active role in implementing their political agenda. The activist character of neoliberal administrations in the United States, the United Kingdom, Australia, and New Zealand during the 1980s and 1990s attests to the importance of strong governmental action in engineering free markets.

> Globalization is about the triumph of markets over governments. Both proponents and opponents of globalization agree that the driving force today is markets, which are suborning the role of government.
>
> *Business Week*, 13 December 1999

> One role [of government] is to get out of the way – to remove barriers to the free flow of goods, services, and capital.
>
> Joan Spiro, former US Under-Secretary of State in the Clinton administration

> The liberal market economy is by its very nature global. It is the summit of human endeavor. We should be proud that by our work and by our votes we have – collectively and individually – contributed to building it.
>
> Peter Martin, British journalist

Moreover, the claim that globalization is about the liberalization and global integration of markets solidifies as 'fact' what is actually a contingent political initiative. Globalists have been successful because they have persuaded the public that their neoliberal account of globalization represents an objective, or at least a neutral, diagnosis of the very conditions it purports to analyse. To be sure, neoliberals may indeed be able to offer some 'empirical evidence' for the 'liberalization' of markets. But does the spread of market principles really happen because there exists a metaphysical connection between globalization and the expansion of markets? Or does it occur because globalists have the political and discursive power to shape the world largely according to their ideological formula:
LIBERALIZATION + INTEGRATION OF MARKETS = GLOBALIZATION?

Finally, this overly economistic representation of globalization detracts from the multidimensional character of the phenomenon. Cultural and political dimensions of globalization are discussed only as subordinate processes dependent upon the movements of global markets. Even if one were to accept the central role of the economic dimension of globalization, there is no reason to believe that these processes must necessarily be connected to the deregulation of markets. An alternative view might instead suggest linking globalization to the creation of a global regulatory framework that would make markets accountable to international political institutions. Yet, for globalists, the presentation of globalization as an enterprise that liberates and integrates global markets as well as emancipates individuals from governmental control is the best way of enlisting the public in their struggle against those laws and institutions they find most restrictive. As long as they succeed in selling their neoliberal understanding of globalization to large segments of the population, they will be able to maintain a social order favourable to their own interests. For those people who remain sceptical, globalists have another claim up their sleeves. Why doubt a process that proceeds with historical inevitability?

Claim 2: Globalization is inevitable and irreversible

At first glance, the idea of the historical inevitability of globalization seems to be a poor fit for an ideology based on neoliberal principles. After all, throughout the 20th century, liberals and conservatives have levelled reasonable criticisms against Marxists for their determinist claims that devalue human free agency and downplay the ability of non-economic factors to shape social reality. Yet, globalists rely on a similar monocausal, economistic narrative of historical inevitability. According to the globalist interpretation, globalization reflects the inevitable spread of irreversible market forces driven by technological innovations. Let us consider the following statements:

> Today we must embrace the inexorable logic of globalization – that everything from the strength of our economy to the safety of our cities, to the health of our people, depends on events not only within our borders, but half a world away . . . Globalization is irreversible.
>
> **Bill Clinton, former US President**

> Globalization is inevitable and inexorable and it is accelerating . . . Globalization is happening, it's going to happen. It does not matter whether you like it or not, it's happening, it's going to happen.
>
> **Frederick W. Smith, Chairman and CEO of FedEx Corporation**

> We need much more liberalization and deregulation of the Indian economy. No sensible Indian businessman disagrees with this . . . Globalization is inevitable. There is no better alternative.
>
> **Rahul Bajaj, Indian industrialist**

The neoliberal portrayal of globalization as some sort of natural force, like the weather or gravity, makes it easier for globalists to convince people that they must adapt to the discipline of the market if they are to survive and prosper. Hence, the claim of inevitability depoliticizes the public discourse about globalization. Neoliberal policies are portrayed to be above politics; they simply carry out what is ordained by nature. This implies that, instead of acting according to a set of choices, people merely fulfil world-market laws that demand the elimination of government controls. As former British Prime Minister Margaret Thatcher used to say, 'there is no alternative'. If nothing can be done about the natural movement of economic and technological forces, then political groups ought to acquiesce and make the best of an unalterable situation. Resistance would be unnatural, irrational, and dangerous.

The idea of inevitability also makes it easier to convince the general public to share the burdens of globalization, thus supporting an excuse often utilized by neoliberal politicians: 'It is the market that made us cut social programmes.' As German President Roman Herzog put it in a nationally televised appeal, the irresistible pressure of global forces demands that everyone will have to make sacrifices. To be sure, President Herzog never spelled out what kinds of sacrifices will await large shareholders and corporate executives. Recent examples, such as the spectacular collapse of Enron Corporation in the United States, suggest that it is much more likely that sacrifices will have to be borne disproportionately by those workers and employees who lose their jobs or social benefits as a result of neoliberal policies.

Finally, the claim that globalization is inevitable and irresistible is inscribed within a larger evolutionary discourse that assigns a privileged position to certain countries at the forefront of liberating markets from political control. As discussed in Chapter 5, optimistic hyperglobalizers often use globalization as a euphemism that stands for the irreversible Americanization of the world. And so it appears that globalist forces have resurrected the 19th-century paradigm of Anglo-American vanguardism propagated by the likes of Herbert Spencer and William Graham Sumner. The main ingredients of classical market liberalism are all present in globalism. We find inexorable laws of nature favouring Western civilization, the self-regulating economic model of perfect competition, the virtues of free enterprise, the vices of state interference, the principle of *laissez faire*, and the irreversible, evolutionary process leading up to the survival of the fittest.

Claim 3: Nobody is in charge of globalization

Globalism's deterministic language offers yet another rhetorical advantage. If the natural laws of the market have indeed preordained a neoliberal course of history, then globalization does not reflect the arbitrary agenda of a particular social class or group. In that case, globalists merely carry out the unalterable imperatives of a transcendental force. People aren't in charge of globalization; markets and technology are. Certain human actions might accelerate or retard globalization, but in the final analysis, the invisible hand of the market will always assert its superior wisdom. Here are three expressions of this view:

Many on the Left dislike the global marketplace because it epitomizes what they dislike about markets in general: the fact that nobody is in charge. The truth is that the invisible hand rules most domestic markets, too, a reality that most Americans seem to accept as a fact of life.

Paul Krugman, US economist

And the most basic truth about globalization is this: *No one is in charge* . . . We all want to believe that someone is in charge and responsible. But the global marketplace today is an Electronic Herd of often anonymous stock, bond and currency traders and multinational investors, connected by screens and networks.

Thomas Friedman, *New York Times* correspondent and
award-winning author

The great beauty of globalization is that no one is in control. The great beauty of globalization is that it is not controlled by any individual, any government, any institution.

Robert Hormats, Vice Chairman of Goldman Sachs International

But Mr Hormats is right only in a formal sense. While there is no conscious conspiracy orchestrated by a single, evil force, this does not mean that nobody is in charge of globalization. The liberalization and integration of global markets does not proceed outside the realm of human choice. As shown in Chapter 3, the globalist initiative to integrate and deregulate markets around the world both creates and sustains asymmetrical power relations. The United States is by far the strongest economic and military power in the world, and the largest TNCs are based in North America. This is not to say that the US rules supremely over these gigantic processes of globalization. But it *does* suggest that both the substance and the direction of globalization are to a significant degree shaped by American domestic and foreign policy.

In short, the claim of a leaderless globalization process does not reflect reality in today's world. Rather, it serves the political agenda of defending and expanding Northern interests while securing the power of affiliated elites in the global South. Like the rhetoric of historical inevitability, the idea that nobody is in charge seeks to depoliticize the public debate on the subject and thus demobilize antiglobalist movements. Once large segments of the population have accepted the globalist image of a self-directed juggernaut that simply runs its course, it becomes extremely difficult to organize resistance movements. As ordinary people cease to believe in the possibility of choosing alternative social arrangements, globalism's capacity to construct passive consumer identities gains even greater strength.

Claim 4: Globalization benefits everyone

This claim lies at the very core of globalism because it provides an affirmative answer to the crucial normative question of whether globalization should be considered a 'good' or a 'bad' thing. Globalists frequently connect their arguments to the alleged benefits resulting from market liberalization: rising global living standards, economic efficiency, individual freedom, and unprecedented technological progress. Here are examples of such claims:

There can be little doubt that the extraordinary changes in global finance on balance have been beneficial in facilitating significant improvements in economic structures and living standards throughout the world . . .

Alan Greenspan, Chairman of the US Federal Reserve Board

Globalization's effects have been overwhelmingly good. Spurred by unprecedented liberalization, world trade continues to expand faster than overall global economic output, inducing a wave of productivity and efficiency and creating millions of jobs.

Peter Sutherland, Chairman of British Petroleum

We are at an optimistic time in our world: the barriers between nations are down, economic liberalism is decidedly afoot and proven to be sound, trade and investment are soaring, income disparities between nations are narrowing, and wealth generation is at record high levels, and I believe likely to remain so.

George David, CEO of United Technologies Corporation

However, Mr David never reveals the ideological assumptions behind his statement. Who exactly is 'we'? Who 'proved' neoliberalism 'sound'? What does 'sound' mean? In fact, however, there exists solid evidence to the contrary. When the market goes too far in dominating social and political outcomes, the opportunities and rewards of globalization are spread unequally, concentrating power and wealth amongst a select group of people, regions, and corporations at the expense of the multitude. Even data taken from the World Bank suggest that income disparities between nations are actually widening at a quicker pace than ever before in recent history.

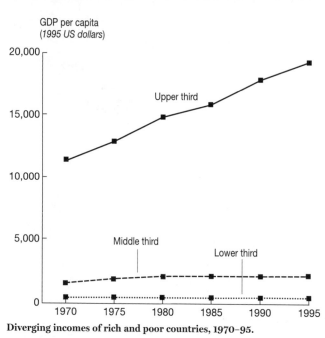

Diverging incomes of rich and poor countries, 1970–95.
Source: World Bank, *World Development Report 1999/2000.*

Data published in the 1999 and 2000 editions of the *UN Human Development Report* show that, before the onset of globalization in 1973, the income ratio between the richest and poorest countries was at about 44 to 1. Twenty-five years later it had climbed to 74 to 1. In the period since the end of the Cold War, the number of persons subsisting below the international poverty line rose from 1.2 billion in 1987 to 1.5 billion today. If current trends persist, their numbers will reach 1.9 billion by 2015. This means that, at the dawn of the 21st century, the bottom 25% of humankind live on less than $140 a year. Meanwhile, the world's 200 richest people have doubled their net worth to more than $1 trillion between 1994 and 1998. The assets of the world's top *three* billionaires are more than the combined GNP of all the least developed countries and their 600 million people.

Map 5. The world by income, 1999.

The same trend towards growing inequality can be observed even in the world's richest countries. Consider, for example, the widening income gap in the United States (see p. 108).

The number of political action committees in the United States increased from 400 in 1974 to about 9,000 in 2000. Such corporate lobbyists successfully pressure Congress and the President to stay on a neoliberal course. Over one-third of the US workforce, 47 million workers, make less than $10 per hour and work 160 hours longer per year than did workers in 1973. The low US

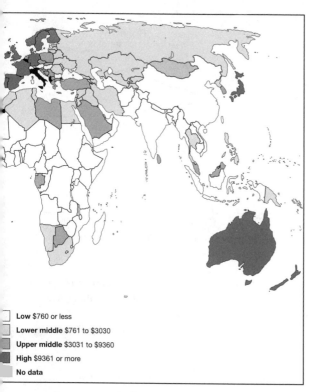

Low $760 or less
Lower middle $761 to $3030
Upper middle $3031 to $9360
High $9361 or more
No data

unemployment rate in the 1990s, often cited by globalists as evidence for the economic benefits of globalization, is masked by low wages and millions of part-time labourers who are registered as employed if they work as few as 21 hours a week and cannot get a full-time job. At the same time, the average salary of a CEO employed in a large corporation has risen dramatically. In 2000, it was 416 times higher than that of an average worker. The financial wealth of the top 1% of American households exceeds the combined wealth of the bottom 95% of households, reflecting a significant increase in the last 20 years.

There are numerous other indications confirming that the global

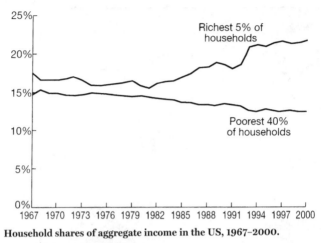

Household shares of aggregate income in the US, 1967–2000.

Source: US Census Bureau, www.census.gov.

hunt for profits actually makes it more difficult for poor people to enjoy the benefits of technology and scientific innovations. For example, there is widespread evidence for the existence of a widening 'digital divide' separating countries in the global North and South.

Global Internet users as a percentage of the regional population, 1998–2000

Country	1998	2000
United States	26.3	54.3
High-income OECD (excl. US)	6.9	28.2
Latin America and the Caribbean	0.8	3.2
East Asia and the Pacific	0.5	2.3
Eastern Europe and CIS	0.8	3.9
Arab states	0.2	0.6
Sub-Saharan Africa	0.1	0.4

| South Asia | 0.04 | 0.4 |
| World | 2.4 | 6.7 |

Source: *UN Human Development Report 2001*.
(OECD: Organization for Economic Cooperation and Development; CIS: Commonwealth of Independent States)

With regard to growing disparities in global health services, consider the story reported by *BBC News* on 31 October 2000:

> A group of scientists in the United States recently warned the public that economic globalization may now be the greatest threat to preventing the spread of parasitic diseases in sub-Saharan Africa. They pointed out that US-based pharmaceutical companies are stopping production of many antiparasitic drugs because developing countries cannot afford to buy them. The US manufacturer of a drug to treat bilharzia, a parasitic disease that causes severe liver damage, has stopped production because of declining profits – even though the disease is thought to affect over 200 million people worldwide. Another drug used to combat damage caused by liver flukes has not been produced since 1979, because the 'customer base' in the global South does not wield enough 'buying power'.

Those few globalists who acknowledge the existence of unequal global distribution patterns usually insist that the market itself will eventually correct these 'irregularities'. They insist that 'episodic dislocations' are necessary in the short run, but that they will eventually give way to quantum leaps in global productivity. In fact, globalists who deviate from the official portrayal of globalization as benefiting everyone must bear the consequences of their criticism. Joseph Stiglitz, the Nobel Prize-winning former chief economist of the World Bank, was severely attacked for publicly criticizing the neoliberal economic policies created by his institution. He argued that the structural adjustment programmes imposed upon developing countries by both the World Bank and the IMF often led to disastrous results. He also noted that 'market ideologues' had used the 1997–8 Asian economic crisis to discredit state intervention and to promote more market liberalization. At the end of 1999, Stiglitz was pressured into resigning from his position. Five months later, his consulting contract with the World Bank was terminated.

Claim 5: Globalization furthers the spread of democracy in the world

This globalist claim is rooted in the neoliberal assertion that free markets and democracy are synonymous terms. Persistently affirmed as 'common sense', the actual compatibility of these concepts often goes unchallenged in the public discourse. Here are three examples:

> The level of economic development resulting from globalization is conducive to the creation of complex civil societies with a powerful middle class. It is this class and societal structure that facilitates democracy.
>
> **Francis Fukuyama, Johns Hopkins University**
>
> The emergence of new businesses and shopping centers in former communist countries should be seen as the backbone of democracy.
>
> **Hillary Rodham Clinton, US Senator from New York**
>
> The Electronic Herd will intensify pressures for democratization generally, for three very critical reasons – flexibility, legitimacy, and sustainability.
>
> **Thomas Friedman, *New York Times* correspondent and award-winning author**

These arguments hinge on a conception of democracy that emphasizes formal procedures such as voting at the expense of the direct participation of broad majorities in political and economic decision-making. This 'thin' definition of democracy reflects an elitist and regimented model of 'low-intensity' or 'formal' market democracy. In practice, the crafting of a few democratic elements onto a basically authoritarian structure ensures that those elected remain insulated from popular pressures and thus can govern 'effectively'. Hence, the assertion that globalization furthers the spread of democracy in the world is largely based on a shallow understanding of democracy.

Moreover, this claim must also contend with ample evidence that points in the opposite direction. Let us consider a report released by the New Economic Information Service cited in the *Chicago*

In 1989, democratic countries accounted for more than half of all US imports from the global South. Ten years later, with more democracies to choose from, democratic countries supplied barely one-third of US imports from developing countries. And the trend is growing. As more of the world's countries adopt democracy, more American businesses appear to prefer dictatorships. These findings raise the important question of whether foreign purchasing and investment decisions by US corporations are actually undermining the chances for the survival of fragile democracies. Why are powerful investors in the rich Northern countries making these business decisions? For one, wages tend to be lower in authoritarian regimes than in democracies, giving businesses in dictatorships a monetary advantage in selling exports abroad. In addition, lower wages, bans on labor unions, and relaxed environmental laws give authoritarian regimes an edge in attracting foreign investment.

Tribune. It suggests that democratic countries are losing out in the race for US export markets and American foreign investments.

Conclusion

A critical examination of the five central claims of globalism suggests that the neoliberal language about globalization is ideological in the sense that it is politically motivated and contributes towards the construction of particular meanings of globalization that preserve and stabilize existing asymmetrical power relations. But the ideological reach of globalism goes far beyond the task of providing the public with a narrow explanation of the meaning of globalization. Globalism consists of powerful narratives that sell an overarching neoliberal worldview, thereby creating collective meanings and shaping people's identities.

Yet, as both the massive antiglobalist protests from Seattle to Genoa and the Al Qaeda terrorist attacks of 11 September 2001 have shown, the expansion of this globalist ideology has encountered considerable resistance. As we shall see in the next chapter, it appears that the first decade of the 21st century is quickly becoming a teeming battlefield of clashing perspectives on the meaning and direction of globalization.

Chapter 7
Challenges to globalism

The dominant ideology of our time, globalism has chiselled into the minds of many people around the world a neoliberal understanding of globalization, which, in turn, is sustained and reconfirmed by powerful political institutions and economic corporations. Yet, no single ideology ever enjoys absolute dominance. Gaps between ideological claims and people's actual experience may usher in a crisis for the dominant paradigm. At such a time, dissenting social groups find it easier to convey to the public their own ideas, beliefs, and practices.

As the 20th century was drawing to a close, antiglobalist arguments began to receive more attention in the public discourse on globalization, a process aided by a heightened awareness of how extreme corporate profit strategies were leading to widening global disparities in wealth and well-being. Between 1999 and 2001, the contest between globalism and its ideological challengers erupted in street confrontations in many cities around the world, climaxing in an unprecedented terrorist attack on the United States that claimed over 3,000 lives. Who are these antiglobalist forces?

Two antiglobalist camps

One sentiment shared by these diverse social forces is their conviction that they must protect themselves and others from the negative consequences of globalization. In this regard, they are all 'protectionists' of some kind. However, it is of the utmost importance to bear in mind that antiglobalist groups pursue a wide range of goals and use different means to advance their political agendas. For example, they differ widely in their respective assessments of the constitutive features of globalization, its causes, and what exactly falls under the category of 'negative consequences'. At the risk of oversimplification, I propose that we divide antiglobalist groups into two large ideological camps, which, in turn, can be further subdivided according to additional criteria.

In the United States, Patrick Buchanan and H. Ross Perot are two prominent representatives of the particularist protectionist position. In Europe, nationalist parties like Jörg Haider's Austrian

Particularist protectionism

Particularist protectionists include groups who blame globalization for most of the economic, political, and cultural ills afflicting their home countries or regions. Threatened by the slow erosion of old social patterns, particularist protectionists denounce free trade, the power of global investors, the neoliberal agenda of multinational corporations, and the Americanization of the world as practices that have contributed to falling living standards and/or moral decline. Fearing the loss of national self-determination and the destruction of their cultures, they pledge to protect their traditional ways of life from those 'foreign elements' they consider responsible for unleashing the forces of globalization. Particularist protectionists are more concerned with the well-being of their own citizens than with the construction of a more equitable international order based on global solidarity.

Freedom Party, Jean-Marie Le Pen's French National Front, and Gerhard Frey's German People's Union have expressed their opposition to 'American-style globalization'. In the global South, one finds similar attitudes in Osama bin Laden's extreme version of Islamism or President Hugo Chávez's Venezuelan brand of national populism. Again, let us keep in mind that these groups must be distinguished not only in terms of their political agendas but also with regard to the means they are willing to employ in their struggle against globalization – means that range from terrorist violence to nonviolent parliamentarian methods.

Universalist protectionism

Universalist protectionists can be found in progressive political parties dedicated to establishing a more equitable relationship between the global North and South. In addition, they include a growing number of non-governmental organizations and transnational networks concerned with the protection of the environment, fair trade and international labour issues, human rights, and women's issues. Challenging the central claims of globalism discussed in the previous chapter, these groups point to the possibility of constructing a new international order based on a global redistribution of wealth and power. Universalist protectionists claim to be guided by the ideals of equality and social justice for all people in the world, not just the citizens of their own countries. They accuse globalist elites of pushing policies that are leading to greater global inequality, high levels of unemployment, environmental degradation, and the demise of social welfare. Calling for a 'globalization from below' favouring the marginalized and poor, they seek to protect ordinary people all over the world from a neoliberal 'globalization from above'.

In the United States, the consumer advocate Ralph Nader has emerged as a leading representative of the universalist protectionist position. In Europe, the spokespersons for established Green parties have long suggested that unfettered neoliberal globalization has resulted in a serious degradation of the global environment. Anarchist groups in Europe and the United States concur with this perspective, but, unlike Nader and the Greens, they are willing to make selective use of violent means in order to achieve their objectives. In the global South, the universalist protectionist perspective is usually represented by democratic-popular movements of resistance against neoliberal policies, such as the Zapatistas in Mexico, the Chipko movement in India, or Haitian President Jean-Bertrand Aristide's poor people's movement. Some of these groups have forged close links to antiglobalist INGOs.

Before we turn to a discussion of major antiglobalist activities in the last few years, let us examine in more detail the most prominent spokespersons of these two antiglobalist camps.

Particularist protectionists

Associated with the right wing of the Republican Party in the United States since the early 1960s, Patrick J. Buchanan sees himself as a patriotic protector of 'hard-working Americans' against corporate elites, recent immigrants, welfare recipients, and minorities enjoying 'special rights'. In recent years, there has been a steep rise in the number of nationalist organizations in America whose antiglobalist rhetoric is even more extreme than Buchanan's nationalism. Groups like the John Birch Society, the Christian Coalition, the Liberty Lobby, and so-called patriot and militia movements are convinced that globalization lies at the root of many social ills in America. Regarding globalism as an alien and godless ideology engulfing their country, they fear that transnational forces are relentlessly eroding the 'traditional American way of life'.

After serious disagreements with leading Republicans on issues of free trade and immigration, Buchanan left his party in 2000 to become the presidential candidate of the populist Reform Party. In his best-selling books and fiery campaign speeches, he refers to his antiglobalist position as 'economic nationalism' – the view that the economy should be designed in ways that serve narrow national interests. He frequently expresses the conviction that there exists at the core of contemporary American society an irrepressible conflict between the claims of American nationalism and the commands of the global economy. In Buchanan's opinion, most mainstream American politicians are beholden to transnational corporate interests that are undermining the sovereignty of the nation by supporting a global governance structure headed by the WTO and other international institutions. He also accuses 'liberal advocates of multiculturalism' of opening the doors to millions of immigrants who are responsible for the economic and moral decline of the United States.

Particularist protectionists in Europe have also warmed to the rhetoric of economic nationalism, which makes it easier for them to

13. Patrick J. Buchanan.

fuel public anxieties over the economic and cultural consequences of globalization. Their targets are international bankers and currency traders, 'footloose capital' and transnational corporations, as well as the EU bureaucracy in Brussels. Considering globalization the greatest threat to national sovereignty and self-determination, right-wing political parties from Spain to Russia are advocating protectionist measures and the re-regulation of international financial markets.

Antiglobalist rhetoric seems to be a particularly effective weapon when combined with the so-called 'foreigner problem'. For many years, the issues of immigration, imported labourers, and the general *Überfremdung* ('over-foreignization') have been important catalysts for the mobilization of public resentment in Austria, Germany, and other European countries, because foreigners represent easily identifiable scapegoats as a threat to the cultural heritage and identity of host countries. Xenophobia usually goes hand in hand with the successful demonization of globalization. European political parties organized around particularist-protectionist themes often attack the globalist claim that globalization is inevitable and irreversible. Echoing Buchanan's language, they call for strong political leaders who would be capable of halting the neoliberal juggernaut. Most of these parties envision the creation of a 'Fortress Europe' consisting of sovereign European nations that would defend their region's political, economic, and cultural independence.

The surge of particularist protectionism in the global North represents an authoritarian response to the economic hardships and cultural dislocations brought about by neoliberal globalization. 'Globalization losers' include industrial workers, small business owners, and small farmers. These groups experience considerable anxiety over the dissolution of secure boundaries and familiar orders. Their political representatives give public voice to the longing for a real or imagined world of cultural uniformity, moral certainty, and national superiority.

Osama bin Laden's radical Islamism, too, harbours a deeply hierarchical and paternalistic streak. Bin Laden projects the image of a charismatic leader and fearless defender of the faith. His religious fundamentalism fuels his struggle against what he considers to be pernicious alien influences. In the Arab world, globalization is usually associated with American economic and cultural dominance. As we noted in Chapter 1, religious organizations like bin Laden's Al Qaeda terrorist network feed on the common perception that Western modes of modernization have not only failed to put an end to widespread poverty in the region, but that they have also enhanced political instability and strengthened secular tendencies in their own societies.

Religious fundamentalism usually begins as a response to what is often experienced as a materialistic assault by the liberal or secular world. Drawing on revivalist themes popularized in the 18th century by theologian Muhammad ibn Abd al-Wahhab, bin Laden and his followers seek to return the Muslim world to a 'pure' and 'authentic' form of Islam – by any means necessary. Their enemies are not merely the American-led forces of globalization, but also those domestic groups who have accepted the alien influences of modernity and imposed them on Muslim peoples. The terrorist methods of Osama bin Laden and his Al Qaeda followers may contradict basic Islamic teachings, but their struggle against globalization finds its ideological sustenance in particularist-protectionist values and beliefs.

Universalist protectionists

A prominent representative of the universalist-protectionist camp in the United States, Ralph Nader enjoys a long-standing reputation as a relentless critic of corporate globalization. By the 1990s, more than 150,000 people were actively involved in his six major non-profit organizations. One of them, *Global Trade Watch*, has emerged as a leading antiglobalist watchdog monitoring the activities of the IMF, the World Bank, and the WTO. During his campaigns for president as the Green Party candidate in 1996 and 2000, Nader presented himself as the protector of democratic principles against the neoliberal forces of globalism. Unlike Buchanan's nationalist version, however, Nader's brand of protectionism refuses to stoke the fires of popular resentment against ethnic minorities, recent immigrants, or welfare recipients. Indeed, he always returns to the idea that globalism must be opposed by an international alliance of egalitarian forces. He also emphasizes that the elimination of poverty and the protection of the environment constitute moral imperatives that ought to transcend the circumscribed territorial frameworks of nation or region.

Nader refuses to accept the globalist claim that globalization equals the liberalization and integration of markets and that this dynamic is inevitable and irreversible. In his view, a successful challenge to

14. **Ralph Nader.**

globalism is possible, but it requires the building of a nonviolent resistance movement across national borders. Rather than emphasizing the central role of strong political leaders, the Green Party candidate invokes the memory of nonviolent social justice movements in the world, in which ordinary people struggled together to overcome steep concentrations of undemocratic power.

Ralph Nader's organizational network in the United States is part of an emerging global web of INGOs whose members believe that people at the grassroots can change the present neoliberal course of globalization. Today, there exist thousands of these organizations in all parts of the world. Some consist only of a handful of activists, while others attract a much larger membership. For example, the *Third World Network* is a non-profit international network of organizations based in Malaysia with regional offices on all five continents. Its objectives are to conduct research on development issues pertaining to the South and to provide a platform for antiglobalist perspectives at international meetings. The *International Forum on Globalization* is a global alliance of activists, scholars, economists, researchers, and writers formed to stimulate a universalist-protectionist response to globalism. Finally, transnational women's networks draw on women's groups from countries around the world to develop common policy initiatives, typically proposals pertaining to women's rights. Given the fact that many victims of neoliberal structural adjustment programmes are women in the global South, it is not surprising to observe the rapid growth of these organizations.

All of these universalist-protectionist networks started out as small, seemingly insignificant groups of like-minded people. Many of them learned important theoretical and practical lessons from antiglobalization struggles in developing countries, particularly from Mexico's Zapatista rebellion. On 1 January 1994, the day NAFTA went into effect, a small band of indigenous rebels calling themselves the *Zapatista Army of National Liberation* captured four cities in the Chiapas region of southeast Mexico. Engaging in a number of skirmishes with the Mexican army and police over the next few years, the Zapatistas continued to protest the implementation of NAFTA and what their leader Subcomandante Marcos called the 'global economic process to eliminate that multitude of people who are not useful to the powerful'. In addition, the Zapatistas put forward a comprehensive antiglobalist programme that pledged to reverse the destructive consequences of neoliberal free-market policies. Although the Zapatistas insisted that a major part of their struggle related to the restoration of the political and economic rights of indigenous peoples and the poor in Mexico, they also emphasized that the fight against neoliberalism had to be waged globally.

The strategy of antiglobalist protectionists in both the particularist and the universalist camp is to challenge globalism in word and action. Throughout much of the 1990s, it seemed as though such antiglobalist efforts were no match for the dominant neoliberal paradigm. However, in the last few years, globalism has come under sustained attack by opponents from both camps.

From the anti-WTO protests in Seattle to the terrorist attacks on the World Trade Center and the Pentagon

A clear indication of an impending large-scale confrontation between the forces of globalism and its challengers came on 18 June 1999, when various labour, human rights, and environmental groups organized international protests known as 'J 18' to coincide with the G8 Economic Summit in Cologne, Germany. Financial districts of cities in North America and Europe were subjected to well-orchestrated direct actions that included large street demonstrations, as well as more than 10,000 'cyber-attacks' perpetrated by sophisticated hackers against the computer systems of large corporations. In London, a march of 2,000 protesters turned violent, causing dozens of injuries and significant property damage.

Six months later, 40,000 to 50,000 people took part in the anti-WTO protests in Seattle. In spite of the predominance of North American participants, there was also a significant international presence. Activists like José Bové, a French sheep farmer who became an international celebrity for trashing a McDonald's outlet, marched shoulder to shoulder with Indian farmers and leaders of the Philippines' peasant movement. Clearly articulating universalist-protectionist concerns, this eclectic alliance of antiglobalists included consumer activists, labour activists (including students demonstrating against sweatshops), environmentalists, animal rights activists, advocates of Third World debt relief, feminists, and human rights proponents. Criticizing the WTO's neoliberal position on agriculture, multilateral investments, and intellectual property rights, this impressive crowd represented more than 700 organizations and groups.

Alongside these groups, however, there also marched a number of people who represented the particularist-protectionist perspective. For example, Pat Buchanan called on his supporters to join the antiglobalist cause against the WTO. Similarly, hard-edged soldiers of neo-fascism, like the Illinois-based 'World Church of the Creator' founder Matt Hale, encouraged their followers to come to Seattle and 'throw a monkey wrench into the gears of the enemy's machine'. Still, it is safe to say that the vast majority of the demonstrators who gathered in Seattle advanced universalist criticisms of free-market capitalism and corporate globalization. Their main message was that the WTO had gone too far in setting global rules that supported corporate interests at the expense of developing countries, the poor, the environment, workers, and consumers.

On the opening day of the meeting, large groups of demonstrators interrupted traffic in the city centre. They managed to block off the main entrances to the convention centre by forming human chains. Many demonstrators who had been trained in nonviolent methods of resistance called for blocking key intersections and entrances in order to shut down the WTO meeting before it even started. As hundreds of delegates were scrambling to make their way to the conference centre, Seattle police stepped up their efforts to clear the streets. Soon they launched tear gas cans into the crowds – including throngs of people who were peacefully sitting on streets and pavements. Having failed to accomplish their goal a few hours later, the Seattle police employed batons, rubber bullets, and pepper spray stingers against the remaining demonstrators. Some police officers even resorted to such methods as using their thumbs to grind pepper spray into the eyes of their victims and kicking nonviolent protesters in the groin. Altogether, the police arrested over 600 persons. Significantly, the charges against over 500 of them were eventually dismissed. Only 14 cases actually went to trial, ultimately yielding ten plea bargains, two acquittals, and only two guilty verdicts.

To be sure, there were perhaps 200 individuals who, having declined to pledge themselves to nonviolent direct action, delighted in smashing storefronts and turning over garbage cans. Most of these youthful protesters belonged to the 'Black Bloc', an Oregon-based anarchist organization ideologically opposed to free-market capitalism and centralized state power. Wearing dark hoods and black jackboots, Black Bloc members damaged stores that had been identified as engaging in extremely callous business practices. For example, they spared a Charles Schwab outlet, but smashed the windows of Fidelity Investments for maintaining high stakes in Occidental Petroleum, the oil company most responsible for violence against indigenous people in Colombia. They moved against Starbucks because of the company's non-support of fair-traded coffee, but not against Tully's. They stayed away from REI stores, but inflicted damage on GAP outlets because of the company's heavy reliance on sweatshops in Asia.

Negotiations inside the conference centre did not proceed smoothly either. Struggling to overcome the handicap of a late start, the WTO

15. Police use tear gas to push back WTO protesters in downtown Seattle, 30 November 1999.

delegates soon deadlocked over such important issues as international labour and environmental standards. Many delegates from the global South refused to support an agenda that had been drafted by the major economic powers behind closed doors. Caught between two rebellions, one inside and one outside the conference centre, officials sought to put a positive spin on the events. While emphasizing the alleged benefits of free trade and globalization, President Clinton nonetheless admitted that the WTO needed to implement 'some internal reforms'. In the end, the meeting in Seattle failed to produce substantive agreements.

Ironically, the Battle of Seattle proved that many of the new technologies hailed by globalists as the true hallmark of globalization could also be employed in the service of antiglobalist forces and their political agenda. For example, the Internet has enabled the organizers of events like the one in Seattle to arrange for new forms of protest such as a series of demonstrations held simultaneously in various cities around the globe. Individuals and groups all over the world can utilize the Internet to readily and rapidly recruit new members, establish dates, share experiences, arrange logistics, identify and publicize targets – activities that only 15 years ago would have demanded much more time and money. Other new technologies, like mobile phones, allow demonstrators not only to maintain close contact throughout the event, but also to react quickly and effectively to shifting police tactics. This enhanced ability to arrange and coordinate protests without the need of a central command, a clearly defined leadership, a large bureaucracy, and significant financial resources has added an entirely new dimension to the nature of street demonstrations.

In the months following the anti-WTO protests in Seattle, several large-scale demonstrations against neoliberal globalization took place in rapid succession all over the world. Here are some of these events:

Washington, DC, April 2000

Between 15,000 and 30,000 antiglobalist activists from around the world attempted to shut down the semi-annual meetings of the IMF and the World Bank. Although most protesters were nonviolent, 1,300 of them were arrested.

Prague, September 2000

About 10,000 protesters attempted to disrupt the annual meeting of the IMF and the World Bank. Street demonstrations turned violent after some marchers had been injured in confrontations with the police. 400 people were arrested.

Davos, January 2001

Antiglobalist forces descended on the World Economic Forum's annual meeting in the Swiss mountain resort. In what has been described as the country's largest security operation since World War II, thousands of police and military units were placed on high alert. Street battles between police and demonstrators led to dozens of injuries and hundreds of arrests. The harsh treatment of peaceful protesters received intense criticism from within Switzerland and abroad.

Quebec City, April 2001

Over 30,000 antiglobalist protesters marched at the Summit of the Americas. Violent street confrontations erupted between police and some demonstrators. Over 400 people were arrested.

London, May 2001

Thousands of antiglobalist protesters marched through London's main shopping area. Disciplined police units and nonviolent demonstrators managed to avoid serious clashes.

Gothenburg, June 2001

Thousands of people demonstrated against globalism at the European Union Summit in Sweden. Peaceful marches turned violent and three protesters were shot with live ammunition. The city's main shopping street was seriously damaged. About 500 people were arrested.

Genoa, July 2001

100,000 antiglobalist demonstrators descended on the G8 Summit in Italy. The protests turned violent when a small group of anarchists got into running battles with police. Dozens of people were injured, and one protester was shot dead by police.

Preparations for similar large-scale demonstrations against the autumn meetings of the IMF and World Bank were underway on 11 September 2001, when three hijacked commercial airliners hit, in short succession, the World Trade Center in New York and the Department of Defense's Pentagon Building in Washington, DC. A fourth plane crashed in Pennsylvania before the hijackers were able to reach their intended target. Over 3,000 innocent people perished in less than two hours, including hundreds of heroic New York police and firefighters trapped in the collapsing towers of the World Trade Center.

In the weeks following the attacks, it became clear that the operation had been planned and executed years in advance by the

16. The burning twin towers of the World Trade Center, moments
before their collapse on 11 September 2001.

Al Qaeda terrorist network. In several videotapes that surfaced in subsequent months, Osama bin Laden left no doubt that his organization had committed these atrocities in response to various manifestations of globalization: the expansion of the American military around the globe, especially the presence of US military bases in Saudi Arabia; the internationalization of the 1991 Gulf War; the escalation of the Palestinian-Israeli conflict; the 'paganism' of the modern world; and the 80-year history of 'humiliation and disgrace' perpetrated against the 'Islamic Nation' by 'international infidels'. Dividing the world's population into 'those who resort to the Almighty' and 'those who refuse to be subdued in His religion', Osama bin Laden's declaration of war against the American-led 'international infidels' embodies the particularist-protectionist impulse in its most extreme form.

No doubt, the events of 11 September 2001 gave an unexpected jolt to the struggle over the meaning and the direction of globalization. As US President George W. Bush made clear in his televised address to Congress nine days after the attacks, the war on terrorism is bound to be a lengthy conflict of global proportions. Will it lead to more extensive forms of international cooperation and interdependence, or will it stop the powerful momentum of globalization? The expansion of the War on Terror to Iraq in Spring 2003 certainly does not seem to bode well for the prospects of enhanced global cooperation. As American and British troops have become bogged down in a lengthy and costly guerilla war, the dark side of globalization – intensifying cultural tensions and growing economic inequality – appears to be gaining the upper hand. Let us turn to the concluding pages of this book for a brief speculation on the future of globalization.

Chapter 8
Assessing the future of globalization

On first thought, it seems highly implausible that even an expanding 'war on terrorism' could stop, or slow down, such a powerful set of social processes as globalization. Yet, there are already some early warning signs. More intense border controls and security measures at the world's major air and seaports have made travel and international trade more cumbersome. Calls for tightening national borders and maintaining sharp cultural divisions can be heard more frequently in public discourse. Belligerent patriotic sentiments are on display all over the world.

A close look at modern history reveals that large-scale violent confrontations were capable of stopping and even reversing previous globalization trends. As we noted in Chapter 2, the period from 1860 to 1914 constituted a 'Golden Age' of globalization, characterized by the unprecedented development of transportation and communication networks, the rapid growth of international trade, and a huge flow of capital. But globalization was capitalistic and imperialistic in character, involving the transfer of resources from the colonized global South in exchange for European manufactures. Great Britain, the world's sole superpower, had spread its political system and cultural values across the globe. However, these sustained efforts to engineer a single global market under the auspices of the British Empire resulted in a severe backlash against globalization that culminated in the outbreak of World War I.

In an important study on this subject, the late political economist Karl Polanyi locates the origins of the social crises that gripped the world during the first half of the 20th century in ill-conceived efforts to liberalize and globalize markets. Commercial interests came to dominate society by means of a ruthless market logic that effectively disconnected people's economic activities from their social relations. The principles of the free market destroyed complex social relations of mutual obligation and undermined communal values such as civic engagement, reciprocity, and redistribution. As large segments of the population found themselves without an adequate system of social security and communal support, they resorted to radical measures to protect themselves against market globalization. Polanyi notes that European antiglobalist movements eventually gave birth to political parties that forced the passage of protective social legislation on the national level. After a prolonged period of severe economic dislocation following the end of the Great War, the particularist-protectionist impulse experienced its most extreme manifestations in Italian fascism and German National Socialism. In the end, the liberal-globalist dream of subordinating the whole world to the requirements of the free market had generated an equally extreme counter-movement that turned markets into mere appendices of the totalitarian state.

The applicability of Polanyi's analysis to the current situation seems obvious. Like its 19th-century predecessor, today's version of globalism also represents a gigantic experiment in unleashing economic deregulation and a culture of consumerism on the entire world. But as we have seen in the previous chapter, the rise of neoliberal globalization has not gone unchallenged. The antiglobalist forces of the 21st century – especially in their violent particularist-protectionist manifestation – seem to be capable of attracting millions of disaffected globalization losers who are willing to employ violent means in order to achieve their political ends. Hence, it is quite conceivable that the Al Qaeda attacks on the World Trade Center and the Pentagon were only the opening salvos of a widening global war waged by the US government and its allies against a growing list of terrorist organizations and their supporters around the world. Such a grim backlash scenario would put the brakes on globalization.

On the other hand, it is also possible that the ongoing efforts to contain these violent forces of particularist protectionism might actually increase international cooperation and encourage the forging of new global alliances. In order to eradicate the primary social causes of terrorism, the global North might be willing to replace the dominant neoliberal version of globalization with a substantive reform agenda designed to reduce the existing disparities in global wealth and well-being. Unfortunately, despite their encouraging reassurances to put a 'human face' on their predatory version of globalization, many globalists have remained within the parameters of their corporate agenda. If implemented at all, their proposed 'reforms' remain largely symbolic in character.

For example, in the wake of the Seattle demonstrations, representatives of the wealthy countries joined the WTO Secretary General in assuring audiences worldwide that they would be willing to reform the economic institution's rules and structure in the direction of greater transparency and accountability. Yet, three years later, no concrete steps have been taken to honour these commitments. Granted, the WTO has been holding special General Council sessions to comply with the urgent requests of developing countries to review several of its questionable procedures. Yet, the spokespersons of the powerful governments in the global North that dominate the WTO have made it clear that they consider existing arrangements as legally binding. In their view, procedural problems can only be addressed in the context of a new, comprehensive round of multilateral negotiations conducted according to the very rules that are being contested by many developing countries and universalist-protectionist organizations.

This new strategy of fortifying the globalist paradigm with a new rhetoric of mild reformism might work for a relatively short period. But in the long run, the growth of global inequality and the persistence of social instability harbours the potential to unleash reactionary social forces that dwarf even those responsible for the suffering of millions during the 1930s and 1940s. Indeed, as recent events have shown, globalization's very survival will depend on its radical transformation. In order to prevent a further escalation of the violent confrontation between globalism and its opponents, world leaders must design and implement a comprehensive 'Global New Deal'.

Serious attempts to build networks of solidarity around the world lie at the very heart of this Global New Deal. The most important element of such a grand bargain must be a sincere commitment on the part of wealthy countries to improve North-South equity. In January 2002, the Summit of the World Social Forum in Brazil – the universalist-protectionist alternative to the neoliberal World Economic Forum in Davos – drew over 50,000 participants who discussed a plethora of specific proposals to transform the current shape of globalization with regard to global governance, social and economic equality, and human rights. Concrete policy proposals included, but were not limited to, the following items that I listed on p. 135.

Without question, the terrorist attacks of 11 September and the ensuing War on Terror in Afghanistan and Iraq have seriously impacted the shape and direction of those social processes that go by the name of globalization. Humanity has reached yet another critical juncture. Lest we are willing to let global inequality climb to levels that virtually ensure new recruits for the violent forces of particularist protectionism, we must link the future course of globalization to a profoundly reformist agenda. As I have

1. A 'Marshall Plan' for the global South that includes a blanket forgiveness of all Third World Debt
2. Levying of a tax on international financial transactions
3. Abolition of offshore financial centres that offer tax havens for wealthy individuals and corporations
4. Implementation of stringent global environmental agreements
5. Implementation of a more equitable global development agenda
6. Establishment of a new world development institution financed largely by the global North through such measures as a financial transaction tax and administered largely by the global South
7. Establishment of international labour protection standards, perhaps as clauses of a profoundly reformed WTO
8. Greater transparency and accountability provided to citizens by national governments and international institutions
9. Making all governance of globalization explicitly gender sensitive.

emphasized throughout this book, there is nothing wrong with greater manifestations of social interdependence that emerge as a result of globalization. However, these transformative social processes must challenge the current oppressive structure of global apartheid that divides the world into a privileged North and a disadvantaged South. If that happens, globalization will have ushered in a truly democratic and egalitarian global order.

References

There is a great deal of academic literature on globalization, but many of these books are not easily accessible to those who are just setting out to acquire some knowledge of the subject. However, readers who have already digested the present volume may find it easier to approach some of the academic works listed below. While these books do not exhaust the long list of publications on the subject, they nonetheless represent what I consider to be the most appropriate sources for further reading. Indeed, my own writing on globalization has greatly benefited from consulting these works. Some of them have influenced the arguments made in the present volume. Following the overall organization of this series, however, I have kept direct quotations to a minimum. Still, I wish to acknowledge my debt to the authors below, whose intellectual contributions to this book are not always obvious from the text.

Chapter 1

Among the most influential academic books on globalization are Anthony Giddens, *The Consequences of Modernity* (Polity Press, 1990) and *Runaway World* (Routledge, 2000); Fredric Jameson and Masao Miyoshi (eds.), *The Cultures of Globalization* (Duke University Press, 1998); David Held, Anthony McGrew, David Goldblatt, and Jonathan Perraton (eds.), *Global Transformations* (Stanford University Press, 1999); Roland Robertson, *Globalization* (Sage Publications, 1992); James H. Mittelman (ed.), *Globalization* (Lynne Rienner, 1996) and *The Globalization Syndrome* (Princeton University Press, 2000); Martin

Albrow, *The Global Age* (Stanford University Press, 1997); Malcolm Waters, *Globalization*, 2nd edn. (Routledge, 2001); and Jan Aart Scholte, *Globalization* (St Martin's Press, 2000).

Manuel Castells' three-volume set, *The Information Age* (Blackwell, 1996–8), constitutes one of the most comprehensive attempts to map the contours of the global information age. Perhaps the most sophisticated critique of globalization theory is contained in Justin Rosenberg's *The Follies of Globalisation Theory* (Verso, 2000). For representative collections of influential essays and excerpts on globalization, see Frank J. Lechner and John Boli (eds.), *The Globalization Reader* (Blackwell, 2000); and Patrick O'Meara, Howard D. Mehlinger, and Matthew Krain (eds.), *Globalization and the Challenges of the New Century* (Indiana University Press, 2000). David Held and Anthony McGrew's *The Global Transformation Reader* (Polity Press, 2000) provides an excellent introduction to the academic globalization debate.

More information on the nature and role of the commercial enterprises mentioned in the chapter can be found on the Internet: www.tbsjournal.com/Jazeera; www.timex.com; www.kalashnikov.guns.ru.

The parable of the blind scholars and the elephant most likely originated in the Pali Buddhist Udana, a collection of Buddhist stories compiled in the 2nd century BCE. The many versions of the parable spread to other religions as well, especially to Hinduism and Islam.

Chapter 2

My discussion in the early part of this chapter has greatly benefited from the arguments made in Jared Diamond's Pulitzer Prize-winning book *Guns, Germs, and Steel* (WW Norton, 1999). I further recommend two general surveys of world history: J. M. Roberts, *A Short History of the World* (Oxford University Press, 1993); and Howard Spodek's college textbook *The World's History*, 2nd edn. (Prentice Hall, 2001).

Held's *Global Transformations* and Scholte's *Globalization* provide useful periodizations of globalization. The best translation of *The Communist Manifesto* can be found in Terrell Carver (ed.), *Marx: Later Political Writings* (Cambridge University Press, 1996).

Chapter 3

Short, accessible introductions to economic globalization include Wayne Ellwood, *The No-Nonsense Guide to Globalization* (New Internationalist Publications, 2001); Sarah Anderson and John Cavanagh with Thea Lee, *Field Guide to the Global Economy* (The New Press, 2000); Kavaljit Singh, *Taming Global Financial Flows* (Zed Books, 2000); and Edward Luttwak, *Turbo-Capitalism* (HarperCollins, 1999). More academic accounts include Robert Gilpin, *Global Political Economy* (Princeton University Press, 2001); Paul Hirst and Grahame Thompson, *Globalization in Question*, 2nd edn. (Polity Press, 1999); Ankie Hoogvelt, *Globalization and the Postcolonial World*, 2nd edn. (The Johns Hopkins University Press, 2001); Will Hutton and Anthony Giddens (eds.), *Global Capitalism* (The Free Press, 2000); and Leslie Sklair, *The Transnational Capitalist Class* (Blackwell, 2001).

An enlightening and very readable study of the Internet's pivotal role in our age of globalization is provided by Manuel Castells in *The Internet Galaxy* (Oxford University Press, 2001).

The best sources for data on economic globalization are the annual editions of the UN *Human Development Report* (Oxford University Press), and the World Bank's *World Development Report* (Oxford University Press).

Chapter 4

David Held's seven points describing the Westphalian model can be found in Held *et al.*, *Global Transformations*, pp. 37–8. My own discussion of political globalization has greatly benefited from insights contained in Chapter 1 of Held's study.

For the arguments of hyperglobalizers, see Lowell Bryan and Diana Farrell, *Market Unbound* (John Wiley & Sons, 1996); Kenichi Ohmae, *The End of the Nation-State* (The Free Press, 1995) and *The Borderless World* (Harper Business, 1990); and Lester Thurow, *The Future of Capitalism* (William Morrow, 1996).

For the arguments of the globalization sceptics, see Ethan B. Kapstein, *Sharing the Wealth* (WW Norton, 1999); Peter Gowan, *The Global Gamble* (Verso, 1999); Daniel Singer, *Whose Millennium?* (Monthly Review Press, 1999); and Linda Weiss, *The Myth of the Powerless State* (Cornell University Press, 1998).

Saskia Sassen's important work on international migration and global cities contains both sceptical and hyperglobalist arguments. See, for example, *Losing Control? Sovereignty in an Age of Globalization* (Columbia University Press, 1996).

On the topic of global politics and governance, see Vincent Cable, *Globalization and Global Governance* (The Royal Institute of International Affairs, 1999); Raimo Väyrynen, *Globalization and Global Governance* (Rowman & Littlefield, 1999); Richard Falk, *Predatory Globalization* (Polity Press, 1999); David Held, *Democracy and the Global Order* (Stanford University Press, 1995); and Daniele Archibugi, David Held, and Martin Koehler (eds.), *Re-Imagining Political Community* (Stanford University Press, 1998).

David Held's elements of cosmopolitan democracy are taken from Daniele Archibugi and David Held (eds.), *Cosmopolitan Democracy* (Polity Press, 1995), pp. 96–120.

Chapter 5
For two comprehensive studies on the cultural dimensions of globalization, see John Tomlinson, *Globalization and Culture* (University of Chicago Press, 1999); and Fredric Jameson and Masao Miyoshi (eds.), *The Cultures of Globalization* (Duke University Press, 1998).

For the arguments of pessimistic hyperglobalizers, see Benjamin Barber, *Jihad vs. McWorld* (Ballantine, 1996); Serge Latouche, *The Westernization of the World* (Polity Press, 1996); and George Ritzer, *The McDonaldization of Society* (Pine Forge Press, 1993).

For the arguments of optimistic hyperglobalizers, see Francis Fukuyama, 'Economic Globalization and Culture: An Interview with Dr. Francis Fukuyama' at www.ml.com/woml/forum/global2.html; and Thomas Friedman, *The Lexus and the Olive Tree* (Anchor, 2000).

For the arguments of the sceptics, see Arjun Appadurai, *Modernity At Large* (Universota of Minnesota Press, 1996); Ulf Hannerz, *Transnational Connections* (Routledge, 1996); and Roland Robertson, *Globalization* (Sage, 1992).

For the role of the media, see Robert W. McChesney and Edward S. Herman, *The Global Media* (Cassell, 1997); and David Demers, *Global Media* (Hampton Press, 1999).

The figures on TV advertising are taken from Television Bureau of Advertising, 'Advertising Volume in the United States', *www.tvb.org*; and Mass Media News, 'Two TV Networks Running 15 Minutes of Ads,', www.taa.winona.msus.edu/mediaupdate/00/11nov.html.

Accessible introductions to globalization and the environment include Hilary French, *Vanishing Borders* (WW Norton, 2000); and Chapter 8, 'Catastrophe in the Making: Globalization and the Environment' in Held *et al.*, *Global Transformations*.

Chapter 6

Portions of this chapter have been adapted from my *Globalism* (Rowman & Littlefield Publishers, 2002). The sources of citations offered in the text boxes of this chapter can also be found in *Globalism*. For additional viewpoints on globalization and ideology, see Pierre Bourdieu, *Acts of Resistance* (The New Press, 1998); Mark Rupert,

Ideologies of Globalization (Routledge, 2000); and Thomas Frank, *One Market Under God* (Doubleday, 2000).

The poll numbers are taken from Aaron Bernstein, 'Backlash: Behind the Anxiety Over Globalization', *Business Week* (24 April 2000): 44. The *Business Week*-Harris poll on globalization was conducted by Harris Interactive 7–10 April 2000. A total of 1,024 interviews were conducted.

Chapter 7

For a more detailed analysis of the two antiglobalist camps, see my *Globalism*, Chapter 4. For readable accounts of various antiglobalist movements and their recent activities, see Alexander Cockburn, Jeffrey St Clair, and Allan Sekula, *5 Days That Shook the World* (Verso, 2000); and Kevin Danaher and Roger Burbach (eds.), *Globalize This!* (Common Courage Press, 2000).

For various perspectives on the role of WTO, see Jeffrey J. Schott, *The WTO After Seattle* (Institute for International Economics, 2000); Sarah Anderson (ed.), *Views from the South* (First Food Books, 2000); and Lori Wallach and Michelle Sforza, *The WTO* (Seven Story Press, 1999).

Chapter 8

For the discussion of the backlash against globalization in the interwar period, see Karl Polanyi, *The Great Transformation* (Beacon Press, 1944). For accessible and detailed descriptions of the reformist agenda, see Hazel Henderson, *Beyond Globalization* (Kumerian Press, 1999); Jeremy Brecher, Tim Costello, and Brendan Smith, *Globalization From Below* (Southend Press, 2000); and Martin Khor, *Rethinking Globalization* (Zed Books, 2001).

Index

Index

Expand your collection of
VERY SHORT INTRODUCTIONS

COSMOLOGY
A Very Short Introduction
Peter Coles

What happened in the Big Bang? How did galaxies form? Is the universe accelerating? What is 'dark matter'? What caused the ripples in the cosmic microwave background?

These are just some of the questions today's cosmologists are trying to answer. This book is an accesible and non-technical introduction to the history of cosmology and the latest developments in the field. It is the ideal starting point for anyone curious about the universe and how it began.

'A delightful and accesible introduction to modern cosmology'

Professor J. Silk, Oxford University

'a fast track through the history of our endlessly fascinating Universe, from then to now'

J. D. Barrow, Cambridge University

www.oup.co.uk/isbn/0-19-285416-X

POSTMODERNISM
A Very Short Introduction
Christopher Butler

Postmodernism has become the buzzword of contemporary society over the last decade. But how can it be defined? In this Very Short Introduction Christopher Butler lithely challenges and explores the key ideas of postmodernism, and their engagement with literature, the visual arts, film, architecture, and music. He treats artists, intellectuals, critics, and social scientists 'as if they were all members of a loosely constituted and quarrelsome political party' – a party which includes such members as Jacques Derrida, Salman Rushdie, Thomas Pynchon, David Bowie, and Micheal Craig-Martin – creating a vastly entertaining framework in which to unravel the mysteries of the 'postmodern condition', from the politicizing of museum culture to the cult of the politically correct.

> 'a preeminently sane, lucid, and concise statement about the central issues, the key examples, and the notorious derilections of postmodernism. I feel a fresh wind blowing away the miasma coiling around the topic.'
>
> **Ihab Hassan, University of Wisconsin, Milwaukee**

www.oup.co.uk/isbn/0-19-280239-9

INTELLIGENCE
A Very Short Introduction
Ian J. Deary

Ian J. Deary takes readers with no knowledge about the science of human intelligence to a stage where they can make informed judgements about some of the key questions about human mental activities. He discusses different types of intelligence, and what we know about how genes and the environment combine to cause these differences; he addresses their biological basis, and whether intelligence declines or increases as we grow older. He charts the discoveries that psychologists have made about how and why we vary in important aspects of our thinking powers.

'There has been no short, up to date and accurate book on the science of intelligence for many years now. This is that missing book. Deary's informal, story-telling style will engage readers, but it does not in any way compromise the scientific seriousness of the book . . . excellent.'

Linda Gottfredson, University of Delaware

'Ian Deary is a world-class leader in research on intelligence and he has written a world-class introduction to the field . . . This is a marvellous introduction to an exciting area of research.'

Robert Plomin, University of London

www.oup.co.uk/isbn/0-19-289321-1

DRUGS
A Very Short Introduction
Leslie Iverson

The twentieth century saw a remarkable upsurge of research on drugs, with major advances in the treatment of bacterial and viral infections, heart disease, stomach ulcers, cancer, and mental illnesses. These, along with the introduction of the oral contraceptive, have altered all of our lives. There has also been an increase in the recreational use and abuse of drugs in the Western world. This book explains what drugs are, how they work, and how medicines are developed and tested. It also discusses current ideas about why some drugs are addictive, and whether drug laws need reform.

'extremely interesting and capable . . . although called a very short introduction, it contains a wealth of information for the interested layman and is exemplary in its accuracy.'

Malcolm Lader, King's College, London

'a slim but assured and wise volume on drugs. [It] takes up many controversial positions . . . with an air of authority that commands respect. It is difficult to think of a better overview of the field for anyone new to it.'

David Healy, University of Wales College of Medicine

www.oup.co.uk/isbn.0-19-285431-3

ANIMAL RIGHTS
A Very Short Introduction
David DeGrazia

Do animals have moral rights? If so, what does this mean?
What sorts of mental lives do animals have, and how
should we understand their welfare? After putting forward
answers to these questions, David DeGrazia explores the
implications for how we treat animals in connection with
our diet, zoos, and research.

'This is an ideal introduction to the topic. David DeGrazia
does a superb job of bringing all the key issues together
in a balanced way, in a volume that is both short and very
readable.'

Peter Singer, Princeton University

'Historically aware, philosophically sensitive, and with
many well-chosen examples, this book would be hard to
beat as a philosophical introduction to animal rights.'

Roger Crisp, Oxford University

www.oup.co.uk/isbn/0-19-285360-0